Rohingyas Displacement Crisis: A Study of RefugeeProtection and Mental Health Issues

LIST OF ACRONYMS:

ACF- Action Against Hunger

GAM- Global Acute Malnutrition

GOM- Government of Myanmar

MOHFW- Ministry of Health and Family Welfare

MHPSS- Mental Health and Psychosocial Support

MSF- Médecins sans Frontières(Doctor without border)

NGO- Non-Government Organization

IASC- Inter-Agency Standing Committee

NLD- National League for Democracy

PTE- Potentially Traumatic Events

PTSD- Posttraumatic Stress Disorder

RA- Research Assistant

RRRC- Refugee Relief and Repatriation Commissioner

SAM- Severe Acute Malnutrition

SGBV- Sexual and Gender-based Violence

UK- United Kingdom

IOM- International Organization for Migration

LSHTM- London School of Hygiene and Tropical Medicine

UNHCR- United Nations High Commissioner for Refugees

UNSW- University of New South Wales

USA- United States of America

WFP- World Food Programme

WHO- World Health Organization

IDP CAMP- Internally displaced person camp

ICRC- International Committee of the red cross

GOB- Government of Bangladesh

OHCHR- Office of the United Nations High Commissioner for Human Rights

CRC- Convention on the Rights of the Child

ICCPR- International Covenant on Civil and Political Rights

CAA- Citizenship amendment act 2019

IMPORTANT JUDGEMENT:

People's Union for Civil Liberties v. Union of India AIR 1997 SC 568

Vishaka v. State of Rajasthan (1997) 6 SCC 241

Vellore Citizens Welfare Forum v. Union of India (1996) 5 SCR 241,

Mohammad Salimulah v. Union of India, Writ Petition (Civil) No. 793 of 2017

Indian Union Muslim League v. Union of India, Writ Petition (Civil) No. 1470 of 2019

Gurunathan and others vs. Government of India

A.C.Mohd.Siddique vs. Government of India

Syed Ata Mohammadi vs. Union of India

Maiwand's Trust of Afghan Human Freedom vs. State of Punjab

Malavika Karlekar vs. Union of India,

State of Arunachal Pradesh vs. KhudiramChakma.

Table of Contents

Rohingyas Displacement Crisis: A study of Refugee Protection and Mental Health Issues

Abstract:

Nearly 86 million people have been forcibly moved around the world as a result of conflict, identity, and violence. The goal of this research is to look into numerous parts and elements of the Rohingya refugee crisis in order to better understand the issues of identity and citizenship, as well as Mental health issues. The Rohingya people of Myanmar stays at Kalandikunj in Delhi.

According to the recent study, India should have a clear policy on refugees, internally displaced persons, and asylum seekers all at the same time. In the case of the Rohingyas, India should likewise address refugee issues in a respectful manner. In addition, the Indian government should assist refugees in returning home freely. This also looks into the refugee's human rights issues.

This research focusses on the Rohingya refugee camps in Delhi, India's capital. It is exploratory and normative qualitative research in nature. The researcher tries to reach a conclusion and gives some recommendations at the end of the study, such as Standard Operating Procedures (Sop's) in Humanitarian Aspects, which every government should follow for the sake of humanity.

In this study, data was acquired by Semi-Structured Interviews and Secondary Data Analysis, with data collected through Purposive Sampling. The study's focus is divided into three main aims. The first is to investigate the root causes of violence against Rohingyas in Myanmar using personal narratives from Rohingyas and key informants' perspectives on the issue. The second is to look into the situation of Rohingyas in refugee camps and the link between mental health and their situation. The last one is to look into the refugee protection gaps and lacunas in India, as well as asylum seeking.

INTRODUCTION

This chapter gives a brief description of the research study conducted on the ongoing 'Rohingya Crisis'. It also explores the domain of statelessness, refugee protection, and mental health issues which plays a pivotal role in the case of Rohingya's who have now fled their homeland in the huge number seeking refuge in neighbouring countries like India and Bangladesh and other southeast nations like Pakistan, Indonesia, and Thailand. The chapter further outlines the chapterization in this research study.

I'm a fly in the kitchen, buzzing

on the boundary of a blind wall.

I'm a chicken under mother's wing,

confined to the narrows of a wattle.

I'm a dove on the street of Yangon,

jailed in the cage of inhumanity.

I'm the water flowing in Mayu river,

missing my partner: Air.

I'm a human in the universe,

denied the most basic rights.

I'm someone I'm afraid of.

BY ZAKI OVAIS

Zaki Ovais, a young Rohingya community development worker, penned the above-mentioned lines. It's the first poetry he's ever written. After an exercise prompting him to contemplate the lyric "I," he wrote the last line, which may be considered his initiation as a poet. Zaki's "I" is confined/jailed/denied in the poem, which reflects the Rohingya's recent past as one of the world's most persecuted ethnic groups.

Myanmar is Southeast Asia's least developed country. The country's name was declared Burma in the 1947 Constitution, but the military regime altered it to Myanmar in 1989. Burma is thought to be derived from the eponym 'Brahma Desha,' after Brahma, one of the Hindu trinity's gods. Other academics claim that the name "Burma" is derived from the spoken form of Bamar (the majority ethnic group's language), and that it was also used during the 1948 independence campaign. The name "Myanmar" comes from the literary version of the language and is thought to be more neutral than "Burma." "Burma" is said to conjure up images of democratic and federalist ideals, whereas "Myanmar" conjures up images of military repression and hierarchical units. According to the 2008 constitution, the country's official name is "The Republic of the Union of Myanmar" Government of Myanmar(GOM), 2008).

Rakhine State(Myanmar) On World Map

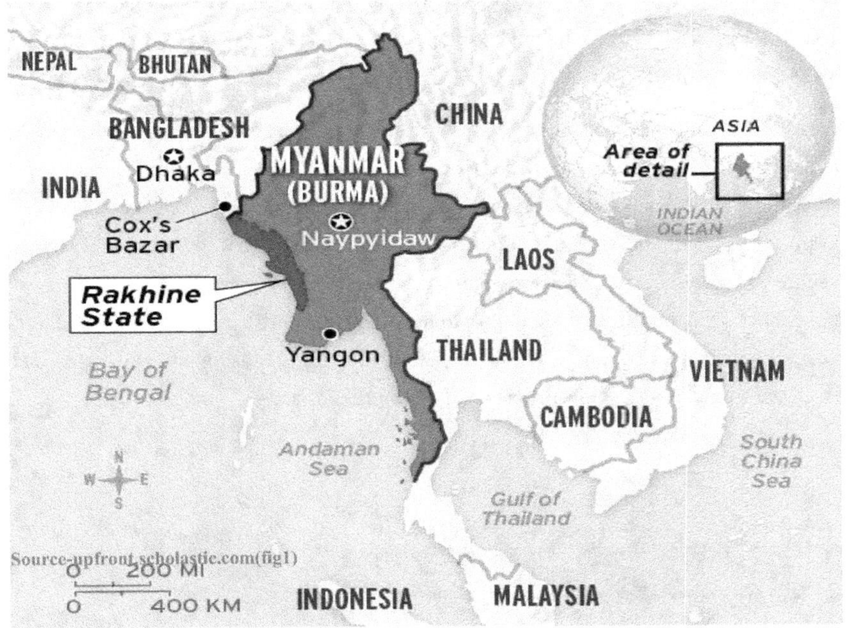

Source-upfront.scholastic.com(fig1)

Rakhine is a state on Myanmar's west coast, and it is one of the country's poorest areas. It has a total size of 14,200 square miles. The Buddhist population of Rakhine is believed to be 59.7%, the Muslim Rohingya population to be 35.6 percent, and the rest to be from other religious groups. The Rohingya Muslims are not descended from a single racial group. They are made up of Arabs, Moghuls, and Bengalis, among other ethnic groups. Myanmar has 7 million Muslims, accounting for 15% of the country's overall population, with Rakhine accounting for half of them.[1]

In response to British colonial authority, Buddhist nationalism arose, with Buddhists identifying with Burmese culture and history. The Burmese military Tatmadaw and the founders of various armies, including Aung San, were patronized and trained by imperial Japan's military to battle Allied forces and British colonial forces during the colonial period. Japanese fascism affected Myanmar's Buddhist nationalism. The Rohingya crisis isn't just about religion; it's also about economic and political issues. Myanmar's Buddhists argue that the Rohingya are economically developed and that their culture is under threat. With Rakhine in Myanmar, the Rohingya are confronted with a deep-seated Islamophobia. Myanmar is bordered on three sides by Islamic countries: Bangladesh, Malaysia, and Indonesia. Buddhists believe that if Myanmar is attacked by an Islamic country, the Rohingya will fight back. As a result, they are subjected to cultural discrimination, economic exploitation, and political marginalization by the GoM.[2]

Armed Rakhine Buddhist persons have destroyed Rohingya villages, homes, and property in northern Rakhine State, according to the Office of the High Commissioner for Human Rights (OHCHR). It also suggests that Rohingyas in Rakhine State are victims of assassinations, kidnappings, torture, rape, and other forms of sexual assault (OHCHR, 2017). The Myanmar government, according to Sanjeev Kumar(Assistant high commissioner of India at Bangladesh), is driving the ethnic Rohingya to flee the nation or risk execution, mass killings, forced labour, and deportation. As a result, Myanmar's Rohingya Muslim minority suffers and faces ethnic cleansing . The Government of Myanmar (GoM) and

---

[1] Jaha, G. (1994). *Rohingya Imbroglio: The Implication for Bangladesh,*
https://jurnal.ugm.ac.id/ikat/article/view/37391
[2] OHCHR(2017) *Myanmar: Report of an Independent International Fact-Finding Mission,*
https://www.ohchr.org/sites/default/files/Documents/HRBodies/HRCouncil/FFM-Myanmar/A_HRC_39_64.pdf

Myanmar Buddhists, treat the Rohingyas as hideous beasts. He has detailed how the GoM was often implicated in ethnic cleansing.[3]

1.1 A History Of Discrimination In Myanmar: The Rohingya

The Rohingya are a Muslim ethnic group who live mostly in western Myanmar's Rakhine State. The vast majority of Myanmar's estimated one million Rohingyas live in Northern Rakhine State, which is generally referred to as Maungdaw and Buthidaung Townships. Amnesty International and other human rights organisations have documented decades of state-sanctioned discrimination and persecution against the Rohingya.[4] The Rohingya have had their citizenship rights revoked, owing to the country's discriminatory Citizenship Law of 1982 and its implementation, as well as violations of their civil, political, economic, and social rights. Following waves of violence between Rakhine Buddhists, Rohingya Muslims, and other Muslim groups in 2012, the Rohingya and other Muslims' position in Rakhine State deteriorated drastically. During the riots, state security forces have also been accused of abusing the Rohingya. Thousands of homes were destroyed and scores of people were killed, resulting in widespread displacement.[5] About 120,000 people, mostly Rohingya, are still living in filthy IDP camps and unauthorised settlements more than four years later. They lack dependable access to proper food, medical treatment, and sanitary services. Government-imposed restrictions prevent displaced individuals from leaving camps, but they also make it difficult for humanitarian agencies to reach the impacted areas.

Outside of the camps, Rohingyas and other Muslims face similar restrictions on their freedom of movement, which limit their access to jobs, healthcare, food, and education. Rohingyas are not permitted to enter the main towns in Central Rakhine State and can only get to Muslim communities via water in most situations. [6]Prior to the October attacks, Rohingya movement in northern Rakhine State was restricted by a complicated system of travel authorizations and

---

[3] "Myanmar Politics and the Tatmadaw(2018)", Directorate of the Public Relations and Psychological Warfare, 2018, p. 116

[4] ICG, Myanmar: Crisis Group Asia Report (15 Dec 2016), A New Muslim Insurgency in Rakhine State

[5] Myanmar: IDP Sites in Rakhine State (Sep 2016), UN Office for the Coordination of Humanitarian Affairs (OCHA), 30 September 2016, available at http://www.refworld.org/docid/58343f474.html

[6] Amnesty international Report on Rohingya persecuted in Myanmar(2017) https://www.amnesty.org/en/latest/news/2017/10/myanmar-new-evidence-of-systematic-campaign-to-terrorize-and-drive-rohingya-out/

limitations imposed by state security personnel, notably the military and Border Guard Police (BGP).

Arbitrary arrests, extortion, torture, and other ill-treatment of the Rohingya population by the BGP have been reported by Amnesty International and other groups. These atrocities are carried out with nearly complete impunity.

Discrimination against the Rohingya has occurred in Myanmar as a result of rising religious intolerance in recent years. Myanmar authorities have generally ignored and disregarded Buddhist extreme groups' advocacy of hatred against Muslims. In recent years, attacks on Muslim communities in numerous parts of Myanmar have resulted in deaths, injuries, and property devastation. After winning a historic general election in November 2015, Aung San Suu Kyi's (NLD) swept to power in March 2016. Aung San Suu Kyi was appointed State Counsellor, a job that made her the de facto leader of the civilian government despite the fact that she is technically excluded from the presidency. She has failed to meet Rohingya and international expectations that she would prioritise the human rights crisis in Rakhine State. Instead, she has attempted to downplay the situation, casting doubt on accusations of abuses against Rohingya Muslims and requesting "space" to resolve the problem. [7]

1.2 An overview of Myanmar's political history, with a focus on the Rohingya:
Historical Development(chronologically):

> Arakan was an independent kingdom that is now known as Rakhine state in Myanmar.
> Arakan people come into touch with Islam through Arab commerce from the **9th to 14th** centuries. Arakan and Bengal have developed close connections.[8]
> **1784:** Arakan is conquered by Burman King Bodawpaya.
> **1824–1942:** Britain conquers Burma (now Myanmar) and makes it a British India province. For infrastructural projects, workers from different parts of British India move to Burma. Burmese Buddhists establish nationalist ideals in the early 1930s.[9] Indians, Chinese, and Muslims are the targets of major riots.

---

[7] Karim, *A 1987 History of Bengal: The Sultani Period*, Dhaka, 2nd Edition (in Bengali)

[8] Nicolaus, P 1995 *'A Brief Account on the History of the Muslim Population in Arakan'*

[9] Maung S L 1989, *Burma: Nationalism and Ideology, University Press Limited, Dhaka*

- ➤ **1942-** Japan invades Burma, driving out the British, resulting in conflict between Buddhists who favour the Japanese and Muslims who support the British.

- ➤ Many Muslims from Arakan flee to East Bengal between **1942 and 1947**.

- ➤ **1945:** With the support of Burmese nationalists, including Muslims, Britain liberates Burma from Japanese domination (Rohingya). The British do not follow through on their promises to provide Arakan autonomy.

- ➤ Freedom from British dominion is granted in **1948**. Tensions between the newly independent Burmese government and the Rohingya, many of whom wanted Arakan to join Muslim-majority Pakistan, are rising. The government retaliates by isolating Rohingya people and expelling Rohingya governmental personnel.

- ➤ **1947:** The Mujahids, a Rohingya militant group, push for an autonomous Muslim homeland in Rakhine. A group of ethnic Rakhine scholars is advocating for the Rakhine people to have their own "Arakanistan."

- ➤ **1962–1974:** General Ne Win and his Burma Socialist Programme Party capture power and adopt a harsh anti-Rohingya stance.

- ➤ The Association of Southeast Asian Nations (ASEAN) is founded in **1967**. Myanmar is not a member because of its "hermit-like" political behaviour, socialist regime, and globally recognised human rights violations.

- ➤ **Between 1974 and 1988**, the Burma Socialist Party (BSPP) is created, completing Ne Win's ideal of a one-party government in which he serves as President.

- ➤ **1977:** Operation Nagamin, or Dragon King, is launched by the military government to screen the population for foreigners. More than 200,000 Rohingya Muslims have fled to Bangladesh, and other parts of the world allegedly due to army brutality.

- ➤ **1977–1978:** The government conducts a nationwide immigration and residence check to eliminate Chinese and Bangladeshi foreigners. Approximately 200,000 Muslims have been compelled to leave the country; practically all of them have been repatriated after establishing their citizenship under current law.

- ➤ **1978:** Bangladesh and Burma reach an agreement for the repatriation of refugees brokered by the United Nations, under which the majority of Rohingyas return.

- ➤ **1982:** A new immigration legislation reclassifies persons who migrated while the United Kingdom was in power as illegal immigrants. The government applies this to all Rohingya, effectively depriving them of their citizenship.

- ➤ **1988:** A second military coup occurs in Myanmar, following years of demonstrations and socioeconomic collapse, resulting in the formation of the State Law and Order Restoration Council.

- ➤ Burma is renamed Myanmar by the army in **1989.**

- ➤ **1990:** General elections are held, with the National League for Democracy (NLD) obtaining 392 seats out of 492; however, the military retains control. Aung San Suu Kyi, the head of the National League for Democracy, and other members of the party have been detained.

- ➤ Over 250,000 Rohingya refugees flee to Bangladesh between 1990 and 1991.

- ➤ **1992–1997** Myanmar and Bangladesh have reached an agreement on voluntary repatriation. Few refugees choose repatriation at first, but the number grows as camp circumstances deteriorate. Approximately 237,000 Rohingya Muslims have returned to Rakhine State. In Cox's Bazar, the UNHCR runs two camps that house around 28,000 registered refugees. Hundreds of thousands of 'unregistered' Rohingya people still live in Cox's Bazar.

- **1997** Myanmar has become a member of ASEAN.

- **2008:** Cyclone Nargis, a significant natural disaster, forces the government to allow more foreign assistance organisations into Myanmar. Initially they are refusing such helps.

- President Thein Sein's Union Solidarity and Development Party (USDP) wins a general election in **2010**. The army (Tatmadaw) is in charge of key government institutions like the Ministry of Home Affairs.

- Parliamentary by-elections are conducted in **2012**. Aung San Suu Kyi is elected to Parliament when the NLD wins a majority of seats. Riots between Rakhine Buddhists and Rohingyas in 2012 resulted in dozens of deaths, the majority of whom were Rohingyas. In Sittwe and the neighbouring districts, about 150,000 people have been driven into IDP camps. Thousands of people are fleeing to Bangladesh.

- The NLD wins by a landslide in the **2015** general elections.

- Harakah al-Yaqin (now known as ARSA), a Rohingya insurgent group, attacks border guard posts in **2016**, killing nine troops. The army strikes back. Around 90,000 Rohingya refugees have fled to Bangladesh. Killings, rape, and arson have all been reported by refugees. The administration of Aung San Suu Kyi rejects the atrocities.

- **2017** In August 2017, a Rohingya terrorist strike in Northern Rakhine State causes widespread violence against Rohingyas, resulting in the migration of almost 1 million Rohingya refugees to Bangladesh.

1.2 <u>The Problem With Rohingyas Citizenships:</u>

The plan to deny Rohingyas citizenship began soon after Myanmar gained independence.[10] In 1948, a Citizenship Act was passed, defining citizenship and recognising specific ethnic groups as indigenous races of Burma, who were authorised to become citizens.The Rohingyas were not mentioned in the list.[11]

"However, the act permitted persons to receive identity cards if they had lived in the country for the preceding two generations." Initially, Rohingyas were given identification cards under this plan, but after the 1962 military takeover, the government began refusing to issue identification cards to Rohingya children, resulting in the complete non-recognition of the new generation of Rohingyas." [12] Later, in 1974, the Myanmar government enacted a new rule requiring all citizens to obtain National Registration Cards, while Rohingyas were only permitted to obtain Foreign Registration Cards, which are not recognised by many employers and schools, severely limiting their employment and educational opportunities. A new citizenship law was enacted in 1982, eliminating the previous one enacted by General Ne Win. "According to the legislation, in order to get citizenship, one must show proof that one's ancestors lived in Myanmar prior to 1948. Many Rohingyas lacked paperwork proving their ancestors' previous residence. As a result, the Burmese government withdrew their ID cards." Even if some of them supplied documentation, they still needed to pass a second level of naturalisation, which required fluency in one of Myanmar's national languages. They were unable to learn one of the national languages due to a lack of educational opportunities.[13]

"National security cannot be put at risk only for humanitarian reasons," General Ne Win defended the action.However, authorization to live in this country is granted by legal processes,

---

[10] Amnesty International, Myanmar(2017): *The ethnic cleansing of Rohingyas in Rakhine State is fueled by a scorched-earth operation. 2017*, https://bit.ly/2wZWZIE.

[11] UNHCR(2016) *Study on Community Perceptions of Citizenship, Documentation, and Rights in Rakhine State, Myanmar*

[12] Rakhine Commission(2017), *For The People of Rakhine, Towards a Peaceful, Fair, and Prosperous Future, Advisory Commission on Rakhine State*, https://www.rakhinecommission.org/app/uploads/2017/08/FinalReport_Eng.pdf

[13] ICG, Myanmar: Crisis Group Asia Report N°282, 15 Dec 2016: *A New Muslim Insurgency in Rakhine State*, https://www.crisisgroup.org/asia/south-east-asia/myanmar/283-myanmar-new-muslim-insurgency-rakhine-state

but government participation is limited. This act has had a significant impact on Rohingyas, who are mostly stateless and unable to seek justice due to a lack of money. Their ethnicity has been denied by government officials on several occasions. Also, one of their foreign ministers, Ohn Gyaw, said that the Rohingya race did not exist in Myanmar and labelled them as illegal immigrants. Their cries are unheard in their nation. Human Rights is dominated by the question of minority rights. International law has traditionally concentrated on this subject and has worked hard to perfect it. Larger challenges, such as apartheid in South Africa, were settled after a lot of fighting and suffering. Similarly, the Rohingyas have concluded their own struggle and now it is time for international authorities to intervene. The Burmese government's purging policy towards Rohingyas must be reversed."

1.4 Social Context of Rohingya Crisis:

Myanmar is a classic example of a fictitious Nations. It is, in fact, a state made up of several nations rather than just one. Many ethnic groups in Myanmar consider themselves not just ethnic minorities, but nations without sovereign states for which they must fight in order to achieve self-determination. According to the Treaty of Westphalia(1648) where The concepts of state sovereignty, mediation between nations, and diplomacy all find their origins in the text of this treaty written more than three hundred and fifty years ago. But Myanmar doesn't fit in the Westphalia model that's why he follow the pollination concept. We define a nation as a group of people who have shared a common history, language, ethnic identity, and culture for a long time and have lived in the same general area. Aside from the majority Buddhist Bama, the Shan, Karen, Rakhine, Rohingya, Kachin, Chin, Karenni, Mon, Wa, and Kokang Chinese are just a few of the countries or ethnic groups in the country. Each of them has a territory that is more or less broadly defined, overlapping at times. Many people follow traditional religions such as Christianity or Buddhism, while others follow traditional religions such as Islam. As a result, Myanmar is a state made up of many nations and religions. Because of the diversity it brings, having a diverse ethnic group or nation is a blessing. At the same time, it is a curse, because these nations' desire for self-determination has resulted in armed conflicts that have lasted until now. Many ethnic groups have armed revolutionary groups fighting the central government, while others have signed ceasefire agreements with it. The majority of Rohingyas are Muslims, with a few Hindus. Many people in Myanmar refer to Rohingyas as "Bengalis" and do not consider them Myanmar citizens.

1.5 Political Context of Rohingya Crisis:

On the one hand, the international community had hoped that Nobel Peace Laureate Aung San Suu Kyi would at the very least take up the Rohingya issue, but she has failed terribly. Ultranationalist groups, on the other side, accuse Aung San Suu Kyi's National League for Democracy (NLD) of failing to promote and safeguard Buddhism. Aung San Suu Kyi is clearly on a tightrope. Many people are curious as to why she has remained silent on the subject. On the one hand, some people outside Myanmar claim that she is complicit in ethnic cleansing. Another explanation is that she is merely a politician, with the military wielding both political and military authority in the country. Who is in authority here: the military or Aung San Suu Kyi? It's unclear what role she plays in this dilemma. The military's relationship with the government may not be straightforward. The reasons for discussion about Aung San Suu Kyi's potential role in settling the Rohingya situation are several. First, she was a symbol of democracy because of her battle for Myanmar people's political rights against the military regime, for which she had been imprisoned multiple times since 1989. Second, she has put her personal life and professional career on hold for the sake of peace. She is also the daughter of Aung San, the founder of modern-day Burma, which is today known as Myanmar. Fourth, she has ties to the University of Oxford. Fifth, she has worked for the United Nations, an organisation dedicated to promoting justice, equality, self-determination, and peace. Sixth, she is a member of the National League for Democracy (NLD), which spearheaded the mass democratic movement that campaigned for the people of Myanmar's democratic rights while the military junta was in power. She is a Nobel Peace Laureate. She has not, however, taken a firm stance in support of the rights of all Myanmar citizens, especially the Rohingya.

1.6 Refugees And The Laws And Conventions That Govern Them:

The study will now go deeper into international conventions that provide refugee protection. Furthermore, there are few case studies that describe their battle and implementation of human rights. In the previous few years, there has been an upsurge of refugee struggle all over the world.

1.7 Refugees Are Defined As:

It was widely believed that defining a refugee was a difficult undertaking. However, in 1951, the United Nations Convention relating to the Status of Refugees (the Refugee Convention) adopted a concrete definition, which states: "owing to a well-founded fear of being persecuted for reasons of race, religion, nationality, membership of a particular social group, or political opinion, is outside the country of his nationality, and is unable to or, owing to such fear, is unwilling to avail himself of that country's protection or return to that country." Persecution of the group should be based on one of the five reasons stated in article 1 A (2) of the Refugee Convention, namely race, religion, nationality, working as a member of a social group, or political opinion.

1. **Race:** A broad term that encompasses ethnic and social groups of shared ancestry.

2. **Religion:** A broader notion that encompasses those who share a common religious heritage and belief.

3. **Nationality** is a term that refers to a person's citizenship. Persecution of ethnic, linguistic, and cultural groupings within a population is also included, as is persecution based on nationality.

4. **A social group** is made up of persons who have a similar background or social standing. This is a category that overlaps with the other four bases; for example, it has been used to families of capitalists, landowners, homosexuals, entrepreneurs, and former military personnel.

5. **Political viewpoint** It is an opinion that the authorities might eventually find intolerable, such as critical analysis of government programmes and tactics. However, it also includes authorities' opinions in cases where they assume a given group of people holds a certain political opinion that they may or may not hold. Those persons are also qualified for refugees who flee their nation because they feel their beliefs will lead to persecution.

1.8 India's Approach to the Rohingyas:

The Rohingya Muslims, who are originally from Myanmar's Rakhine State, have long been targets of the government. The Buddhist majority state has committed horrific atrocities against the Rohingya Muslims, including mass massacres, persecution, and sexual assaults. The violence began in 2012 and became more intense in 2017-18. Since then, millions of Rohingya Muslims have sought sanctuary in Bangladesh, India, Malaysia, Thailand, and Indonesia, among other countries. The United Nations has also dubbed them the "world's most persecuted minority" (Human Rights Council, 2017; UNHCR, n.d.).

The Rohingya Muslims' plight has worsened since escaping to India, where they are trapped in a cycle of persecution that leads to statelessness and abandonment. The persecution of Rohingya refugees in India is based on their faith. Right-wing Hindutva trolls have accused Rohingya Muslims of being agents of Islamic terrorism and of carrying out terrorist attacks in places of India.[14] Hindu right-wing media outlets have concocted intricate conspiracy theories linking Rohingyas to ISIS and Lashkar-e-Taiba. The generic labelling of Rohingya Refugees as "terrorists" is plainly related to their Muslim religion connection. The current study focuses on the data surrounding the entry of Rohingya refugees in India and the Indian government's response.[15] The report also examines India's duty under international law to safeguard Rohingya refugees, highlighting how the Indian government has disregarded its international commitment to protect them through the Citizenship Amendment Act, 2019 (CAA).

1.9 Data:

The State of Myanmar had a population of 54 million people as of 2019 (World Bank, 2019). According to estimates, roughly 1.3 million Rohingyas live in Myanmar, out of a total population of 54 million. Several Rohingya communities have fled to Bangladesh and India as a result of the persecution. An estimated 40,000 Rohingyas sought asylum in India, according to the Indian Home Ministry and Reuters[16]. UNHCR India acknowledged the presence of

---

[14] Chaudhury Basu Ray, (2020). *The ruling of the International Court of Justice (ICJ) on the Rohingya people and its ramifications. The Observer Research Foundation provided the information for this article.*
[15] S. Haidar (2017, Sep 09). *The move in Bali positions India on the other side of the Rohingya issue.* The following is an expert from The Hindu:
[16] India (2020, March 17). In the case of Indian, *Union of India vs Union Muslim League, Writ Petition (Civil) No. 1470 of 2019*

18,000 Rohingyas in India in January 2019. (UNHCR India, 2019). This means that some Rohingyas in India have been living in exile for a long time and are still stateless and statusless.

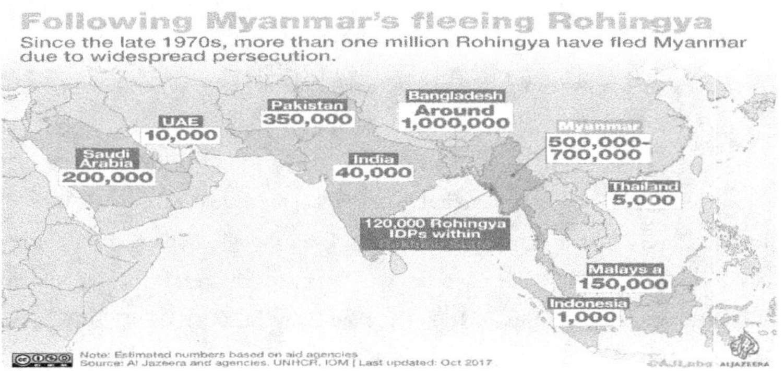

1.10 Obligations of India under International Law:

India does not recognise the UNHCR's Refugee Cards because it is not a signatory to the 1951 Refugee Convention. This means that Rohingyas living in India have no special rights to rations, jobs, housing, or education. As a result, the vast majority of Rohingyas are thought to work in rag-picking, unskilled, and unstructured jobs.[17]

While India is not a party to the 1951 Refugee Convention or the 1967 Refugee Protocol, it is a signatory to a number of core treaties that require states to ensure that all people have access to basic human rights and dignity, as well as to provide basic protection to people seeking asylum in India. The Universal Declaration of Human Rights (UDHR) of 1948, for example, allows people the right to seek asylum in other countries if they are persecuted in their own country [Article 14]. Similarly, the International Covenant on Civil and Political Rights (ICCPR), the Convention on the Elimination of All Forms of Discrimination Against Women (CEDAW), and the Convention on the Rights of the Child (CRC) all provide affirmative rights to ensure dignity, respect for life and liberty, and a healthy environment for children. All three conventions are signed by India, and Article 51(c) of the Indian Constitution instructs the

---

[17] R. Baker (2010). *Old, Challenges and New, Debates in Customary International Law in the Twenty-First Century*, (page 172-203) in The European Journal of International Law, vol. 21, no. 1.

government to "promote respect for international law and treaty responsibilities in the dealings of organised peoples with one another." Indian courts have construed the Fundamental Rights enshrined in Part III of the Constitution in accordance with international law in a number of judgements. The Supreme Court of India concluded in People's Union for Civil Liberties v. Union of India AIR 1997 SC 568 that the ICCPR's provisions are immediately enforceable in India and can be utilised to carry out the Constitution's provisions.

The Supreme Court ruled in **NHRC vs Arunachal Pradesh** that the state is obligated to defend the life and liberty of every human being, citizen or not. Even though, India is unwilling to accept and assist Rohingya refugees. The importance of voluntary nature of repatriation was emphasised in **P. Nedumaran vs. Union of India**, and the Court held that the UNHCR, as a global agency, was to ascertain the voluntariness of the refugees, and that it was not for the Court to consider whether consent was voluntary. The Supreme Court of India adopted the complete CEDAW into Indian law in another decision, **Vishaka v. State of Rajasthan (1997) 6 SCC 241**. Furthermore, in **Vellore Citizens Welfare Forum v. Union of India (1996) 5 SCR 241**, Customary International Law was determined to be immediately integrated into domestic law in the absence of any contrary legislation. Nonetheless, the Indian government's approach to providing Rohingyas with safety and assistance falls short of its international obligations and responsibilities. It is claimed that the neglect of Rohingya refugees is primarily motivated by religious prejudice, and that it is in line with the Indian government's increasing discrimination and persecution of its own Muslim minorities.

1.10 <u>Neglect and Discrimination on the Basis of Religion: A Timeline:</u>

Date	Event	Explanation
08 August 2017	The Centre has ordered states to identify and expel foreign nationals who are residing in the country illegally.	The Home Ministry assigned authority for identifying anddeporting unlawful immigrants to state governments in its recommendationNo.24013/29.'Misc./2017-CSR.III(i). The states were also ordered to "sensitise all law enforcement and intelligence services." Security issues were further exacerbated by "infiltration" from Myanmar, according to the report. **States do not have the authority to expel asylum seekers without first considering their individual and collective circumstances. The concept of non-refoulment is violated by such deportations.**
06 September 2017	Prime Minister Narendra Modi has expressed his "alarm" about "extremist violence" in Rakhine State (The Wire, 2017)	We share your worry about security officer dying in the line of duty and innocent people due to extremist violence in Rakhine state," Prime Minister Modi stated during his visit to Nay Pyi Taw. In his speech, Prime Minister Modi backed the Myanmar government's stance on Rohingyas, ignoring the country's widespread human rights violations and humanitarian catastrophe.

08 September 2017	India refuses to sign Bali Declaration	The World Parliamentary Forum's common statement was rejected by India. The statement expressed worry about the Rohingya Muslims' killings and fled. India vetoed it, claiming that the session was supposed to be about SDGs, not country-specific clauses.
09 September 2017	During his visit to Myanmar, the Indian Ministry of External Affairs issued a statement (Government of India, 2017)	"Terrorist attacks on Myanmar security forces in Rakhine State" were fiercely condemned by India. According to the statement, during the Prime Minister's visit on September 6, 2017, he pledged to help the Rakhine State Development Programme. The statement makes no mention of India's assistance to Rohingya Muslims or its disapproval of Myanmar's mistreatment of them.
14 September 2017	Initiation of Operation Insaniyat by the Indian Government (Government of India, 2017)	Bangladesh received assistance from India in hosting a significant number of Rohingya Muslims. It offered food kits and other requirements in order to take advantage of Bangladesh's position as a host country. The Indian government has not provided food or other basics to Rohingya refugees who have arrived in India.
15 March 2018	In the name of 'National Interest,' India denied that its Border Security Forces are forcing back refugees and denying recognition to Rohingya Muslims.	In the matter of Mohammad Salimulah v. Union of India, Writ Petition (Civil) No. 793 of 2017, a petition was filed in the Supreme Court seeking recognition and protection for Rohingya Muslims in India. The Border Security Forces are "doing their duty" to promote India's security by preventing Rohingyas from entering without passports,

		according to an affidavit filed on behalf of the Union of India. The petition was refused since the submission was solely based on newspaper articles. The document further claims that the increased number of Rohingyas is the "fundamental cause of terrorism's spread."
04 October 2018	The Supreme Court has dismissed a petition to halt the deportation of seven Rohingya Muslims (The Indian Express, 2018).	In reaction to the first incident of Rohingya deportation, the Supreme Court stated that it is "not willing to interfere" with the Central Government's decision. The Supreme Court's decision failed to accept the international law's responsibility to protect.
12 December 2019	Enactment of the Citizenship Amendment Act (CAA), 2019	People who arrived in India from Afghanistan, Bangladesh, or Pakistan before December 31, 2014 and who are Hindu, Sikh, Buddhist, Jain, Parsi, or Christian can apply for fast-track citizenship under the newly enacted CAA. While the Act is marketed as a refugee policy by India's Home Minister, it excludes Muslims, including Rohingya refugees. It is argued that the Act infringes on the right to equality guaranteed by Article 14 of the Indian Constitution.
03 January 2020	The Indian Express (2020) reports on plans to expel Rohingya Muslims from India.	Following the adoption of the CAA, Union Minister of State in the Prime Minister's Office Dr. Jitendra Singh stated that the Central Government was "considering options" to deport the Rohingya Muslims. The CAA, he explained, does not award citizenship to Muslim refugee seekers. The

		Rohingya Muslims would be repatriated to Myanmar as a result. The CAA, he continued, applies in the Union Territory of Jammu and Kashmir, which has a sizeable Rohingya population.
17 March 2020	The terms "Rohingya," "Ethnic," and "Persecution" are all mentioned by India.	In their counter-affidavit in the case of Indian Union Muslim League v. Union of India, Writ Petition (Civil) No. 1470 of 2019, India finally admitted that Rohingya Muslims endure ethnic persecution. However, it was claimed that these asylum seekers came to India rather than Bangladesh in search of work.

The sequence of significant responses reveals that the state has failed to recognise and act on its international legal responsibility to protect, instead erecting sociocultural and legal barriers to Rohingya refugees' presence and reception in India. The BJP-led government changed the Passport Act of 1967 and the Foreigners Act of 1946 in 2015 to make it illegal for Muslims to enter India without a passport or seek refuge. The Citizenship Amendment Act (CAA) of 2019 reiterates the position of the Indian government from 2015.[18] Anti-Muslim legislation, such as the CAA, has fostered terror in the minds of not only Rohingya Muslims, but also Muslims living in India. In an interview with the Anadolu Agency, Ali Johar, a young Rohingya leader, stated that the CAA has fostered terror in the minds of Rohingya Muslims, and that over 3000 people have fled to Bangladesh to avoid harsh vilification and deportation because they are Muslims (Kapoor, 2020). Many people, he added, have considered changing to another religion. Minorities' fear of state tyranny collided with the mainstream narrative.[19]

---

[18] Kinseth, A. S. (2019, January 29). *India's Rohingya shame*. Retrieved from Aljazeera: https://www.aljazeera.com/opinions/2019/1/29/indias-rohingya-shame/

[19] L. Mewara, (2019). *Deportation of Rohingyas is illegal under international law and in India's legal precedents*. The following is an excerpt from The Wire. https://thewire.in/law/deportation-rohingya-supreme-court

1.11 __Mental Health Issue of Rohingya Refugees:__

This research examines the factors that contribute to mental health issues among Rohingya refugees and asylum seekers in India, as well as the challenges that care providers face. As a result, it draws attention to a variety of interventions that are needed to help Rohingya refugees deal with their mental health issues. This includes the MHPSS framework's holistic framework of action, which includes pharmacotherapy, psychological interventions, and psychosocial support, as well as policy advocacy and cultural competency capacity building for agencies working with the Rohingya in order to develop long-term solutions. Overall, more research is needed to fill the information void that currently exists.

As a result of prior human rights violations, including violence in Myanmar, Rohinya refugees today face harsh living conditions in Indian and Bangladeshi refugee camps. Movement limitations, a lack of livelihood options, issues meeting basic necessities, safety concerns, and limited access to services like as healthcare and education are among the challenges in the camps, as documented elsewhere. Conditions have deteriorated in recent months as a result of Covid19 and related steps to slow transmission, as well as seasonal extreme weather events creating flooding and other problems.

Mental health issues have been exacerbated by Myanmar's history of brutality and systemic human rights violations, as well as daily stressors connected with refugee living in Bangladesh.

High degrees of despair, anxiety, PTSD, anger, psychosomatic symptoms, and suicide tendency are all examples of this. Unfortunately, due to resource limits and other challenges, such as a lack of trained mental health staff who can speak the Rohingya language, there are impediments to addressing population-level mental health issues, resulting in a lack of scaled culturally relevant therapies.[20]

As the Rohingya refugee problem has grown in size in recent years, demand has mounted to find long-term solutions. To date, the main focus has been on repatriating Rohingya refugees to Myanmar; however, as several stakeholders have pointed out, the situation is not yet favourable to a safe return. Despite this, Bangladesh and Myanmar agreed to a contentious repatriation framework, with preparations in place to repatriate the first batch of families

---

[20] UNHCR(2018) *Cox's Bazar, Strategic plan for Mental Health and Psychosocial Support (MHPSS) for UNHCR's Rohingya Refugee Response* – 2018,
https://www.scirp.org/(S(351jmbntvnsjt1aadkozje))/reference/referencespapers.aspx?referenceid=2823272

without consulting the community or the UNHCR. These repatriation plans have been viewed as inappropriate in the present political atmosphere after the Myanmar military throw the democratic government in February 2021 making debates about the prerequisites for a safe and voluntary return all the more important.[21] Post-traumatic stress disorder (PTSD) is a mental health illness brought on by watching or experiencing a horrific incident. Flashbacks, nightmares, and acute anxiety, as well as uncontrollable thoughts about the event, are all possible symptoms. Most people who experience traumatic events have temporary difficulties adjusting and coping, but they normally get better with time and adequate self-care. You may have PTSD if your symptoms worsen, linger for months or even years, and interfere with your day-to-day functioning. It's crucial to get treatment as soon as PTSD symptoms appear in order to lessen symptoms and enhance function.

---

[21] Human Right Watch(2017), *All of my body was in pain: Sexual abuse against Rohingya women and girls in Burma*, Human Rights Watch, https://www.hrw.org/sites/default/files/report_pdf/burma1117_web_1.pdf

CHAPTER 2

METHODOLOGY

The research's rationale, objectives, and questions are presented in this chapter. It also includes details about the study's research site and methods. The procedures for selecting samples, sampling, and data collection are comprehensively presented, with special emphasis on the tool, technique, scope, and limitations of the study. In addition, there is a lot of discussion on reflection and research ethics. Overall, the chapter was able to provide an in-depth explanation of the ever-logical procedures taken to complete the research.

2.1 Rationale of The Study:

Myanmar's government has purposefully excluded Rohingya Muslims. The government's and political leaders' allegations that Rohingyas are illegal migrants are unjustifiable, given that they have been a part of Burma's lengthy history. This population group has been systematically marginalized, persecuted, denied basic rights, and abused as a result of exclusionary policies. Due to unwillingness to sign the 1951 Convention and a lack of national legal frameworks in most Southeast Asian nations, the available protection space for Rohingya refugees in the region has become exceedingly unpredictable. Despite political pressure from the international world and local activist groups urging the government to cease the killings, no signs of an end to the violence have emerged.

The goal of this research is to evaluate the links between systematic human rights violations, traumatic experiences, daily stressors, and mental health symptoms. Distance and lack of communication with families in the home country and/or asylum-seeking nations also contribute to mental health difficulties, such as survivor guilt and financial security, as a result of trauma. As well as water and sanitation sites, children are at risk of starvation, trafficking, and becoming ill with covid 19 or other illnesses. Even India maintains that the Rohingyas are a threat to national security and have ties to international terrorist organisations. While advocating for eventual repatriation, Bangladesh and its international partners should look beyond short-term planning and collaborate to provide secure housing, boost refugee educational and livelihood prospects, and support refugee-hosting communities. Rohingya refugees are among the world's most vulnerable individuals. One of my friends recommended that I view the documentary "Myanmar's Killing Fields (2018)" on the Rohingya people. I was stunned when I saw this. According to the report, Myanmar accounted for 1.1 million of the world's refugees at the end of 2018, following a harsh government campaign on the Rohingya Muslim minority. This documentary, based on hidden footage shot by a network of citizen activists, exposes the narrative of a coordinated operation against Rohingya Muslims in majority-Buddhist Myanmar that began more than five years ago, long before their departure made international headlines. In the film, Rohingyas living in Bangladesh's world's largest refugee camp tell terrible stories of why they fled. Mumtaz Begum, who survived a massacre in the village of Tula Toli, said, "My five-year-old was tossed into the river." "I was carrying a two-year-old child on my hip." They snatched the infant from his mother and hurled him into the fire... My kid was wailing as they raped me, so they macheted her three times."

2.2 <u>Objectives of The Research:</u>

(1) To analyze and understand the Rohingya displacement and related citizenship issues in Myanmar.

(2) To understand the nature of displacement and asylum-seeking in India.

(3) Examine the condition of Rohingyas in refugees' settlement and understand the relation of mental health.

(4) To analyze the refugee protection gaps and lacuna.

2.3 <u>Research Questions:</u>

1) What are the geneses and historical backgrounds of the Rohingya refugees?

2) Who is Responsible for the Rohingya Crisis and what is the Role of UNHRC?

3) what are the various problem faced by Rohingya in India? Their reason for refugees in India?

4) What is the role of different Profit and Non-profit Organizations, working for the Rohingya refugee in India?

5) How do we ensure Displaced Rohingya Children and Women at high risk for a mental health problem in Refugee Camp?

6) What are the Indian Government's views toward Rohingyas living in Delhi? With special reference to National Security?

7) What is the legal status of the Rohingyas and analyze the refugee protection gaps and lacuna?

2.4 <u>Methodology:</u>

To gain a holistic understanding of the research questions. It is critical to develop and implement a research strategy. It is vital to ensure that procedures are dependable and can be validated while doing so. The study uses a qualitative research design to acquire a complete understanding of the research issues. Both primary and secondary data are used in the book. For primary data, qualitative semi-structured interviews with fieldwork and policy experts working in reputable think tanks, as well as a few Rohingya refugees living in Indian refugee camps, were chosen. A substantial portion of the secondary material used in the research came from journal papers, monographs, newspaper research, UN and Human Rights Watch publications; numerous websites such as The Foreign Affairs, Diplomat, Dawn, Hindu, and others will be used as a point of reference. The term 'research methodology' refers to a 'method for solving the research problem in a methodical fashion.' It's been described as a "science of analysing how scientific research is conducted." It entails a study of the numerous procedures and methods that a researcher must follow in order to investigate a research problem, as well as the reasoning behind them.

2.5 <u>Research Site:</u>

"The physical, social, and cultural environment where the researcher performs the study is referred to as a research context." The focus of qualitative research is mostly on meaning-making, and the researcher observes the participant in his or her natural environment." The research was carried out in Delhi's Kalindi Kunj.

Delhi- The city's cultural and racial diversity gives refugees an edge in the city, as refugees do not stand out as a separate group among the city's residents, who come from all across India. Delhi also has a growing number of upwardly mobile young adults who are eager to try new cultures and cuisines. Refugees fill this void since the media exoticizes their identity, generating greater interest in their ethnic cuisine. The Rohingya Refugees looked to be the most integrated among the refugees I met, in terms of being happy and financially better off than when they initially arrived in Delhi.

The traditional ethos of welcoming visitors and supporting people seeking refuge works well in Delhi. This culture is maintained through mythology and folklore, and sheltering refugees is associated with the virtue of magnanimity. Despite the fact that India is neither a signatory to the 1951 Refugee Convention or the 1967 Protocol, refugees have always been welcomed in India – until the current surge of religious nationalism. Because there was no formal refugee policy, government actors were able to be more flexible in their treatment of migrants, based on their own personal opinions and convictions. I strongly hope that this period of religious nationalism passes without inflicting extra pain to Indian refugees, and that we can continue to welcome our visitors as we have done in the past.

2.6 An Example of The Location Description:

Kalandi Kunj(Delhi): I am introducing a place with a relevant example. It doesn't take long for news from Rakhine, Myanmar's western coast, to reach a Rohingya refugee camp in Kalindi Kunj, a neighborhood on New Delhi's southeastern outskirts bordering the Yamuna river.

Google Earth map of Kalandi Kunj Refugee Camp

Google Earth Map of Kalandi Kunj(Madanpur Khadar) Refugee Camp

Here live stateless Rohingya refugees. The land they live on was given to them by the Zakat Foundation, an NGO dedicated to uplifting Muslim communities around the world. When these refugees arrived in India in 2012 and protested outside the UNHCR, asking for assistance and support, the property was offered to them. In June 2012, the Zakat Foundation of India donated a block of land approximately 1,100 square yards in Madanpur Khadar, New Delhi, for the rehabilitation of Rohingya refugees. The Zakat Foundation of India has set an example not only in India, but around the world, by giving this land to Rohingya refugees. Thousands of people throughout the world help refugees, but most of their assistance is limited to providing food, clothing, and temporary shelter for a brief time.

Darul Hijrat, in Kalandi Kunj, is home to about 50 Rohingya families.

Despite its large oil resources, Rhakine is the second poorest state in Myanmar. According to Dr. Syed Zafar Mahmood, President of India's Zakat Foundation, the economic issues at hand are key to understanding the origin of the problem.

The bamboo homes in Darul Hijrat caught fire in the early hours of April 15, 2018. There were no casualties or injuries, thanks to God's grace. However, the hutments and the refugees' goods were destroyed by fire. 'Who lit the cabins on fire,' a reporter asked ZFI. He was told by Zfi that no proof or circumstantial indications of sabotage had been discovered. The ZFI was tasked with making alternative arrangements for the refugees' lodging and sustenance. In the long run, if the government granted special permission, ZFI will gladly develop multi-story buildings on this land so that the Rohingya families and their generations have the same fundamental living conditions as other human beings.

After Fire ZFI(Zakat Foundation Of India) construct new Camps:

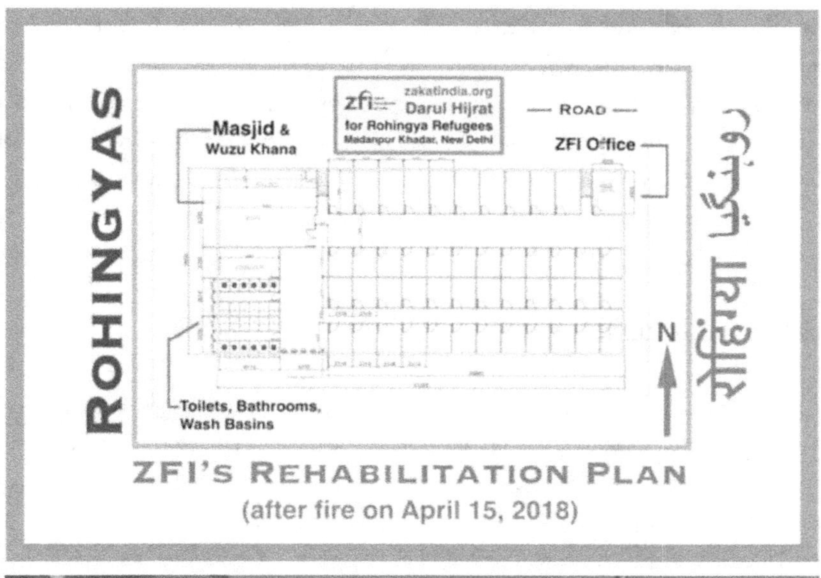

Following the fire, ZFI launched a social media campaign to raise funds for those who had been rendered homeless and impoverished as a result of the blaze. However, following a fire, ZFI always create measures for their rehabilitation. Some have claimed that the Rohingya deserved the fire because they lived in crowded slums, and that they had brought this disaster upon themselves in this way.

We responded that they had no choice but to live in slums since they faced torture, incarceration, and death in their nation, and the Indian government refused to provide them with any services or protection because they were not recognised as refugees. Others were more forthright. India, according to some, is not a dharmsala. India should not squander its resources on undesirable visitors. It should refuse to vaccinate them as well. It should simply evict them and return them to Myanmar. Others stated that they were radicalised terrorists and needed to be deported to "radical Muslim countries."

The refugee's main occupations are day labourers, vehicle drivers, and a few who are better off owning a modest shop providing daily necessities. In addition, the settlement contains a tiny mosque and a small madrassa where people can pray. They live in a makeshift structure composed of bamboo, wood, ply, and plastic sheets. These houses are in close proximity to one another and lack sufficient ventilation, natural light, electricity, and other amenities. Although the water quality is exceedingly poor and unsafe for human consumption, the residents of this village share shared restrooms and three hand-pumps for water supply. Furthermore, there is a lack of basic sanitation and cleanliness in the neighbourhood.

2.7 Research Design:

The word "research design" refers to the whole planning and execution of a research endeavour. It is the process of visualizing the full qualitative research process prior to the start of the investigation. Because every research study is built on the existing stock of our knowledge, the design adopted is exploratory. The existence of adequate knowledge is essential for the formulation of the Issues, stating the study's objectives, and formulating the hypothesis, if necessary. Qualitative Analysis, This style of research is diametrically opposed to quantitative research. It seeks answers to "What's" and "How's" and is explanatory in character. It largely focuses on why a theory exists and what the respondent's reaction would be to it. This allows a researcher to make an informed decision based on correct data. In qualitative research, case studies are frequently utilised to better comprehend societal nuances. The fundamental goal is to investigate the problem, comprehend it, analyse many elements of the situation, and lastly propose long-term remedies.

2.8 Sampling:

The terms 'sample' and 'population' are interchangeable. The universe or population refers to the total group from which the sample is drawn, while the group that is actually chosen for a study is referred to as the sample.

2.9 Snowball Sampling:

In this study, the Snowball Sampling method will be applied. The researcher has identified one or more individuals from the population of interest, and participants will be contacted according to a pre-determined contact schedule. The respondents will be identified using the close network of refugees living in the camps. They were used as informants after being interviewed to identify other members of the population, who were then used as informants, and so on. When it's difficult to identify members of a population, such as when it's a clandestine group, snowball sampling comes in handy.

2.10 Participants In The Research:

Participants in the study were separated into two groups. Subjects of Research and Experts in the Field of Research The research subjects are the people who the study revolves around. They are an important part of the data collection process because the research focuses on their problems. Their feedback is critical in determining the applicability of existing laws, enforcement agency tactics, and, ultimately, the impact on their lives and livelihood. Research experts are experts in the field of research who are well-known for their expertise and experience in the field. Their contributions are critical in identifying and understanding legal gaps and restrictions, as well as creating long-term remedies.

2.11 Research Participant:
Include Rohingya refugees living in Kalandi Kunj camps in Delhi.

Research Experts:

i. Field Officer Of ZFI

ii. Government Officer

iii. Doctors who are working for Rohingya Refugee

iv. NGO: Zakat Foundation Of India

Size of A Sample

Subjects will be selected from a refugee camp of at least 12 refugees and 1 to 2 specialists from each category.

Sample Universe:

The sample of refugees so taken is from Kalandi Kunj in Delhi, because of the complicated adverse situation Present in the Refugee camp. The research apart from focusing on the refugees will also focus on data collected from NGO's, UNHCR Websites, Books and Different News Articles. Therefore, the universe is Delhi, Refugee camp in Kalandi Kunj and the experts will be met in Delhi.

2.12 **Data Collection Tool**:

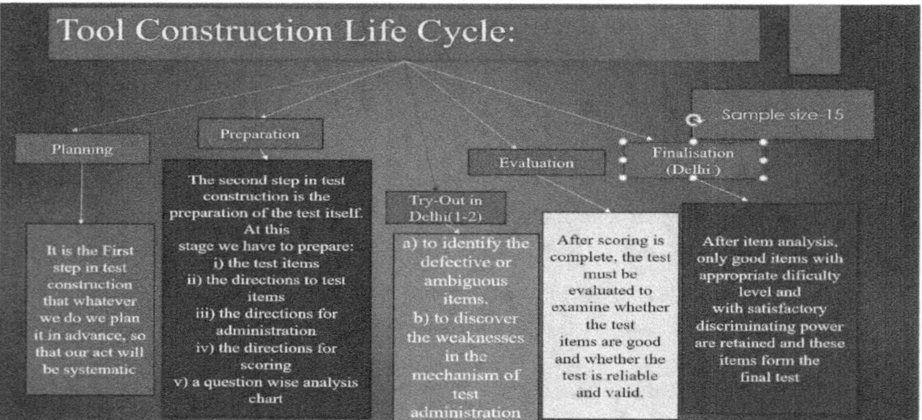

The study comprises an interview guide for experts and Rohingya refugees. These interviews will be semi-structured, and non-participant observation will also be employed as a data gathering strategy. Primary data will be collected through field observations and semi-structured interviews with both experts and subjects, with the interview schedule for each being distinct. Secondary data gathering methods will be used to acquire data from secondary sources and other research materials.

Semi-structured Interviews: Interviews are undertaken to obtain individual experiences or Perspectives, various thoughts, experiences, and the causes for subjective behaviour." It has a lot of the unstructured interviewing quality that is based on the usage of an interview guide. This is a list of questions and subjects that must be addressed in a specific order." The semi-structured interview is made up of a series of straightforward questions that are asked in a conversational tone.

The interview guide's structure is flexible. Although the sequence is variable, the researcher is expected to have a set of questions and should not go to the field without a list of subjects to cover. This type of interviewing strategy is very useful when dealing with persons who are pressed for time during an interview. Daily wage workers, diplomats, and officials are among them. The interviewees are Rohingya refugees living in various camps in Delhi, as well as professionals in the field of study from the aforementioned organisations.

2.13 Pilot Study:

A pilot study could not be delivered to the refugees, the Research Subjects, due to a lack of time and restricted access to refugee camps. As a result, a pilot was done by giving the interview guide to the Field Officer at the NGO's office, such as ZFI. This research was carried out to determine the effectiveness of the Interview Schedule that had been established, and suitable changes were made to the Schedule based on the Schedule's deficiencies in order to make it more effective before it was used in the above-mentioned Camps.

2.14 Analytical Techniques:

During the interviews, a mobile phone was utilized as a recording device, which aided in the preparation of the study's transcript. Only my mentor and I had access to the notes taken during the interviews and nonparticipant observation. The voice media files and notes are kept private in order to protect the identities of informants who do not want to be identified. In addition, the respondent was provided an informed consent statement that explained the study's specifics and obtained their consent.

2.15 Scope of The Research:

There is a clear gap in academic research on Rohingya statelessness and citizenship denial, particularly in the Indian academic sector. As a result, this study aims to identify the causes of statelessness among Rohingya refugees, as well as the dynamics of being compelled to flee and seek asylum, the daily struggle for survival, and the dread of expulsion that these refugees experience. As a result, understanding the many areas of refugeeness becomes vitally important. Similarly, the required aspect entails examining the changes that have occurred in these individuals' lives without overlooking the issue of inequity in service delivery to them. When dealing with such difficulties, it is equally critical to comprehend the political implications on a local and worldwide level. Overlooking either component could result in a disaster, so coming up with long-term solutions that are agreeable to all parties is a good idea. There are also alternative methods for resolving ethnic and religious conflicts, such as communication and understanding the reasons for the conflict's occurrence in order to eradicate it. Stigmatization and marginalisation of these people should be avoided at all costs; the very least that might be done is to ensure that they have a safe place to live, eat, and sleep. On the grounds of humanitarian assistance, these cannot be denied.

2.16 <u>Limitation of The Research Process:</u>

Previous studies and news articles on Rohingya refugee camps in and around Delhi were able to provide sufficient information on the data site, making the data gathering process go smoothly. Establishing trust with the refugees, on the other hand, was a huge challenge in terms of gathering quality data on the effects that refugees encountered as a result of the illegal use of material by various media outlets. The refugees' initial refusal to cooperate was justified solely on the grounds that their truth might be corrupted throughout the research's later stages. Their doubts were dispelled by authentic documentation (identity card and research letter), and they were able to gladly engage in the study. Rohingya Refugees are split into two or three large family bundles in the camp, and camp has a community head with whom authorization to conduct interviews must be secured. The most important barrier in the research study was a language barrier, despite the fact that their (refugee) experience in India had clearly prepared them to grasp a big portion of the dialogue. Due to the pervasiveness of patriarchy in the society, women participants were unwilling to participate in the data collection procedure. Furthermore, many male immigrants were unavailable for late-day interviews since they were daily wage workers who needed to go out throughout the day to find work.

2.17 <u>Research Ethics:</u>

While conducting the research, the researcher has used the cooperative procedure, which ensures that this research is solely for academic reasons. Before beginning his data collection, the researcher has ensured that the necessary approvals are secured, as required by law, and that the laws are followed throughout. When interviewing the participants in the research, consent has been requested to record all of the data. When exposing data, the researcher has protected the utmost secrecy of the participants, and only after consulting the guide will any material be published or documented as part of the book work. The researcher had not, under any circumstances, mislead or misrepresent oneself to the research participants. Because a portion of the research had conducted in refugee camps, the researcher has ensure that the refugees' daily activities has not be disrupted. The researcher has not, under any circumstances, engage in any illicit actions (such as bribery) during the course of the research.

2.18 <u>CHAPTER PLAN:</u>

I. INTRODUCTION

II. RESEARCH METHODOLOGY

III. REVIEW OF LITERATURE

IV. STUDY OF POST DISPLACEMENT TRAUMA

VI. CONCLUSION AND WAY FORWARD

REVIEW OF LITERATURE

In order to provide a comprehensive knowledge of the subject examined, the current chapter seeks to review the literature around the topic from various secondary sources such as books, newspaper articles, academic publications, and Documentary on refugees and statelessness authored by specialists and researchers. This chapter is an important element of the research study since it discusses numerous aspects related to the research study's topic utilising both theoretical and empirical material that is organised thematically.

Review of Books

Review of Reports

Articles

Documentary

3.1 REVIEW OF BOOKS:

3.1.1 "The Rohingyas: Inside Myanmar's Genocide" Authored by Azeem Ibrahim:

Azeem Ibrahim's book The Rohingyas: Inside Myanmar's Hidden Genocide is an engaging and endearing account of the Rohingyas' persecution in Myanmar. This book provides an excellent grounding and foundation for understanding the Rohingya Muslim minority group and their struggle for recognition among Myanmar's 135 ethnic groups for scholars who want to know "who are the Rohingya." Ibrahim has meticulously documented the Rohingya's agonising plight, culminating in the government of Myanmar's brutal genocide. The Rohingyas also provide valuable insight into the difficulties faced by a Rohingya, who are widely regarded as intruders from across the border in both Myanmar and Bangladesh. The Rohingya, a stateless

Muslim minority from Myanmar's Rakhine State, are estimated to number around one million people today. As a result, they are denied land and property rights and ownership, and the land they live on can be taken away at any time by the government. In fact, Myanmar regards them as illegal immigrants, a perception that stems from their ancestors' origins in East Bengal, now Bangladesh.

The book The Rohingyas is divided into seven chapters, the first three of which trace the Rohingyas' history and the origins of their persecution. The city grew to be one of Asia's richest and attracted a large number of migrants due to its location on the border between Buddhist and Muslim Asia. The Rakhine Kingdom, however, fell under the control of the Kingdom of Burma in 1785, which was absorbed into British India. During colonial times, the Muslim community in Rakhine grew rapidly, more than doubling in size between the 1880s and the 1930s. The Rakhine State was on the front lines between Japanese troops and Allied forces during WWII, and it was here that the first substantial divisions between future Burmese communities emerged. While the majority of Muslims were pro-British, the Rakhine Buddhists originally supported the Japanese. A Muslim uprising arose in Rakhine shortly after Myanmar gained independence from British domination, with the intention of establishing an autonomous area for themselves and equal rights with the Buddhist ruling classes. The insurgency was finally crushed, resulting in the establishment of military authority in the region, and any rights that the Rohingya had before to the battle were undermined. The problem has only gotten worse since then. Between 1978 and 1991, government-led campaigns drove over 200,000 Muslims across the border into Bangladesh. Despite the passage of new citizenship regulations that identified 135 national ethnic groups, the Rohingya were not one of them. In reality, they were left effectively stateless.

In chapter 4, Book describes Myanmar's efforts to impose 'social control' on the Rohingya, as well as the consequences for the increasingly predominantly disgruntled people. The Rohingya were omitted from Myanmar's first census in more than three decades. Even in the first democratic elections since the end of military rule, Rohingya Muslims were barred from running for office or voting. The persecution of the Rohingyas spiralled out of hand after Aung San Suu Kyi became the de facto leader in a power-sharing agreement with the military. The Myanmar military carried out periodic crackdowns on the Rohingya, resulting in an estimated mass migration of 87,000 Rohingyas, predominantly to Malaysia and Bangladesh. Despite the fact that the military portrayed the situation as a series of 'clearing operations,' the crackdowns included countless examples of savage torture, rape, murder, and the razing of towns. Despite

Suu Kyi's condemnation of human rights violations, Myanmar's military has denied carrying out atrocities against the Rohingya.

Chapter 5 examines why the international community and civilian sectors of Myanmar's government mostly declined to assist and support the people during the 2012 ethnic cleansing. The book really shines here by explaining the benefits and drawbacks of genocide in Myanmar. The Rohingyas help us comprehend the difficulties of political involvement, the role of the media and freedom of the press in publicising human rights violations, and the issue of government corruption. Ibrahim also explained the politics behind Burma's democracy, emphasising that a state-controlled election would not be able to solve the country's political, economic, or social problems. Finally, chapters 6 and 7 depict the current situation in Myanmar and explain what should be done to bring it under control. Ibrahim did an excellent job of evaluating how the international community may play a key role in Myanmar's reconciliation process.

The Rohingyas is a meticulous chronicle of one of the world's worst humanitarian crises. Ibrahim also addresses the important question of why, despite numerous reports of human rights violations and a refugee crisis, the government has yet to resolve the issues at the heart of the Rohingya's plight. Furthermore, the Association of Southeast Asian Nations (ASEAN) and the International Criminal Court (ICC) have both failed to provide justice to the people persecuted in Rakhine state. Ibrahim concludes by arguing that, as Myanmar makes a slow transition to democracy, it must remember that democracy's success is dependent on the people's inclusive mindset and genuine participation in the new political system. However, with the military and corrupt demagogues wielding so much power, it appears that the Rohingya's precarious situation and troubles are only the beginning.

3.1.2 First, They Erased Our Name-A Rohingya Speaks Authored by Habiburahman:

Habiburahman grew up in a tiny town in western Burma, where he was born in 1979. The country's military head said when he was three years old that his people, the Rohingya, were not one of the 135 ethnic groups that comprised the eight 'national races.' In his own country, he was left stateless.

As a result of tremendous prejudice and persecution, millions of Rohingya have been forced to escape their homes since 1982. In 2016 and 2017, the government accelerated its ethnic cleansing campaign, forcing over 600,000 Rohingya Muslims to flee to Bangladesh.

For the first time, a Rohingya speaks up in order to reveal the truth about the worldwide humanitarian situation. I learn about the Rohingya people's history of persecution through the eyes of a child.

3.1.3 Karim, A 1987 History of Bengal: The Sultani Period, Dhaka, 2nd Edition (in Bengali and Translated into English):

For much of the 14th, 15th, and 16th centuries, the Sultanate of Bengal (Bengali: Saltanat-e-Bangl) was an empire located in Bengal. With a network of mint towns strewn over the Ganges–Brahmaputra Delta, it was the region's preeminent force. Odisha in the southwest, **Arakan** in the southeast, and the Bengal Sultanate had a ring of vassal states. This book also shaw the significance of the Rohingya peoples and his presence in the particular region.

3.1.4 Nicolaus, P 1995 'A Brief Account on the History of the Muslim Population in Arakan:

According to The Nicolaus The first settler in Arakan were the Kanran, a tibeto-burman tribe. Migration down from the Himalayan mountains, they and related tribes occupied the Chittagong Hills and subsequently also the Arakan region. The first Muslim who arrived in Arakan were Arab sailor who settled along the coast in the 8th and 9th centuries. Their numbers were small and, mixing with the local population, they and their offspring soon their lost his identity. The first large wave of Muslims arrived in Arakan in the 15th century. In 16th centuries muslim were backbone of the Arakan.

3.1.5 (Mimeo) Maung S L 1989, Burma: Nationalism and Ideology, University Press Limited, Dhaka:

What happens in Burma has far-reaching consequences for people in South and Southeast Asia. A former Burmese guerrilla and social concerns are discussed in this book. He links its origins to Burmese people's historical and cultural diversity, the country's feudal and colonial background, and the turbulent whirlwind of modern political ideas.

Burma, according to the writers, is at a crossroads between Ne Win's socialism, the Burma Communist Party's communism, the Federation of Burma's democracy, and the breakup of the current area into feudal republics. Shew Lu Maung explores all of the issues in detail and provides readers with useful knowledge about Burma.

3.1.5 The Plight of the Stateless Rohingyas: Responses of the State, Society & the International Community By Imtiaz Ahmed:

The analysis indicates that the Rohingya refugee problem was formed over the course of numerous historical trajectories in tracing the predicament of the Rohingya refugees. The Rohingyas have been proven to be both stateless and refugees. They first became stateless in their own country, then were forced to accept refugee status in the face of persecution, prejudice, and torture. Despite their refugee status, the Rohingya refugees in Bangladesh have remained stateless. Primary factors (as defined in the 1951 Convention), secondary factors (as defined in the 1969 OAU Convention), and auxiliary factors are the causes of their refugee status (such as economic, ecological and demographic change). Denial of citizenship rights, restrictions on movement, eviction campaigns, forced labour, displacement from their homes and lands, brutality, and physical torture all contributed to the Rohingyas becoming stateless and refugees. As this study shows, refugees encounter a variety of psychosocial and human security challenges. This study recognised four primary components of security: politico-military, economic, social, and environmental.

3.1.6 Being Stateless and the Plight of Rohingyas By Kaveri:

Citizenship is a requirement of fundamental human rights. It entails a level of safety. It gives you a sense of self-identity and belonging. It is empowering and promotes growth. However, in recent decades, the global burden of conflicts within national borders has become the dominating reality with which states and humanitarian organizations must contend. This growing problem has resulted in a rapid increase in statelessness and refugee population migration, culminating in flagrant violations of people' and communities' human rights. The majority of these conflicts included long-term state-sanctioned violence along ethnic–religious lines. The ethnic Rohingyas, a minority Muslim population in Myanmar (Burma), are one such example.

3.2 <u>REVIEW OF REPORT:</u>

3.2.1 Rohingyas: The Emergence of a Stateless Community A Report by Calcutta Research Group(Mahanirban,2017):

Before their borders divided them into separate independent nations, India, Bangladesh, and Myanmar were historically unified or closely linked. The boundaries separating these territories, on the other hand, have mostly remained porous, and the more governments attempt to secure them, the more migration, whether legal or illegal, occurs. As a result, it's not unexpected that Rohingyas from Myanmar cross the Naf River into Bangladesh in quest of a safe haven in a climate of "well-founded fear of persecution." On the other side, the Rohingyas' second and third generations, who have already established themselves in Bangladesh's refugee camps and makeshift settlements, are crossing the sea in search of work in Southeast Asian countries. Over the high seas, Rohingyas are travelling not only as asylum seekers, but also as economic migrants from Bangladesh to Southeast Asian countries. As a result, migration has a mixed nature. Despite the considerable risk of travelling in ramshackle boats with the help of middlemen, the water appears to be more accessible than land. They're also smuggled to Southeast Asia, West Asia, and Australia. It's important to emphasise how dangerous their search for a more secure territory was. It has put them in border detention facilities, where they are frequently on the verge of death, or forced them into bonded labour. The 'pull factors,' as they're known.

3.2.2 Rohingyas in India: The Birth of a Stateless Community Report by Mahanirban Kolkata

From December 2015 to December 2016, CRG undertook a year-long research initiative on the Rohingya Refugees in India under the supervision of the Distinguished Chair Prof. Ranabir Samaddar.

The findings of the six scholars, including Sucharita Sengupta, were published in a report titled "Rohingyas: The Emergence of a Stateless Community," which was coordinated by Professor Ranabir Samaddar and Professor Sabyasachi Basy Ray Chaudhury, Vice Chancellor, Rabindra Bharati University. Three scholars performed fieldwork in West Bengal Correctional Homes and Rohingya camps in North and South India in July 2015, while two researchers based their fieldwork in Bangladesh. The draught papers were originally given on March 19, 2015, during a research session on "Interrogating Forced Migration," and the final papers were delivered on August 13-14, 2015, in Darjeeling. The report, based on extensive field research in portions of India and Bangladesh, focuses on the Rohingyas' history and current status, as well as their recent plight as 'boat people' within the broader context of statelessness in South Asia. On December 1, 2015, the Indian Society of International Law (ISIL) in New Delhi released this study. It was later released to the press in Kolkata on 9 February 2016, at the American Centre's Lincoln Room. Three of Kolkata's main print media outlets covered the report's release. Aside from the Report, a publication called Policies and Practices (number 71) was also released as part of the project. Individual articles written by project researchers have been published in media outlets like as Anandabazar Patrika, Hardnews, and others.

3.2.3 Report of the independent international fact-finding mission on Myanmar:

In its decision 34/22, the Human Rights Council created an international fact-finding mission on Myanmar. Since 2011, the mission has been concentrating on the situation in the states of Kachin, Rakhine, and Shan, as per its mandate. It also looked into violations of fundamental freedoms, such as freedom of expression, assembly, and peaceful association, as well as the issue of hate speech. In the states of Kachin, Rakhine, and Shan, the mission discovered a pattern of serious human rights breaches and abuses, as well as major violations of international humanitarian law. Myanmar's security personnel, mainly the military, are the main perpetrators. Their activities are predicated on policies, techniques, and behaviour that routinely violate international law, including attacking civilians. Many of the violations are classified as international crimes of the highest severity. Given the entrenched culture of impunity on the domestic level, the mission concludes that international pressure for accountability is required. It makes specific recommendations to that aim, including the investigation and prosecution of specified senior Myanmar military generals for genocide, crimes against humanity, and war crimes before an international criminal tribunal.

3.2.4 The Displaced And Stateless Of Myanmar In The ASIA-PACIFIC Region Published By UNHCR:

By the middle of 2020, UNHCR estimated that there were 1.9 million Myanmar refugees in the Asia-Pacific area. The Rohingya, a minority community from Myanmar who have been forcibly relocated across the region, made up the vast majority (about 1.6 million). Myanmar's discriminatory citizenship laws have deprived nearly all Rohingya people of their citizenship, making them the world's biggest stateless people.

Nearly one million Rohingya refugees and asylum seekers have been registered by the UNHCR, predominantly in Bangladesh (860,000), Malaysia (101,000), and India (18,000), with lesser numbers in Indonesia, Nepal, Thailand, and other countries. An estimated 600,000 Rohingya people remain in Myanmar's Rakhine State, with 142,000 of them internally displaced.

3.2.5 Rohingyas in India Reported by Stichting the London Story(Ngo):

The Rohingya Muslims, who are originally from Myanmar's Rakhine State, have long been targets of the government. The Buddhist majority state has committed horrific atrocities against the Rohingya Muslims, including mass massacres, persecution, and sexual assaults. The violence began in 2012 and became more intense in 2017-18. Since then, millions of Rohingya Muslims have sought refuge in Bangladesh, India, Malaysia, Thailand, and Indonesia, among other countries. They've also been dubbed the "world's most persecuted minority" by the United Nations (Human Rights Council, 2017; UNHCR, n.d.). The Rohingya Muslims' plight has worsened since escaping to India, where they are trapped in a cycle of persecution that leads to statelessness and abandonment. The persecution of Rohingya refugees in India is based on their faith. Right-wing Thinker trolls have accused Rohingya Muslims of being agents of Islamic terrorism and of carrying out terrorist attacks in places of India. Right-wing media outlets have concocted intricate conspiracy theories linking Rohingyas to ISIS and Lashkar-e-Taiba. The generic labelling of Rohingya Refugees as "terrorists" is plainly related to their Muslim religion connection. The current study focuses on the data surrounding the entry of Rohingya refugees in India and the Indian government's response.

3.2.6 Culture, Context And Mental Health Of Rohingya Refugees Published By UNHCR:

There is a scarcity of information about the Rohingya's culture and mental health, which providing Mental Health and Psychosocial Support (MHPSS) and related services to them difficult. As a result, UNHCR commissioned this report with the goal of providing a comprehensive review of the research on Rohingya refugees' culture, background, mental health, and psychosocial well-being.

The document's content is based on a thorough study of the published and unpublished literature, as well as information provided by UN agencies, non-governmental organisations, and states. Published and unpublished archival data, academic publications, records, and other relevant documentary materials from fields such as anthropology, ethnocultural studies, psychology, and public health were included in the search. After an advanced copy was sent out for extensive discussion among academics, NGO employees, and UN specialists, a core group of multidisciplinary professionals created and reviewed draught versions of the document.

3.2.7 Amnesty International, Myanmar:. The ethnic cleansing of Rohingyas in Rakhine State is fueled by a scorched-earth operation. 2017:

New information obtained by Amnesty International points to a large-scale scorched-earth campaign in northern Rakhine State, in which Myanmar security forces and vigilante mobs are burning down entire Rohingya communities and murdering civilians at random as they attempt to leave.

The organization's analysis of extreme fire data, photographs, satellite imagery, and well as interviews with dozens of eyewitnesses videos from the ground, as well as interviews with dozens of observers in Myanmar and Bangladesh, shows how an orchestrated campaign of systematic burnings has targeted Rohingya villages across northern Rakhine State for almost three weeks.

"The evidence is irrefutable: Myanmar security forces are deliberately setting fire to northern Rakhine State in an attempt to drive the Rohingya people out of Myanmar." "Make no mistake: this is ethnic cleansing," Amnesty International's Crisis Response Director, Tirana Hassan, stated.

3.2.7 Final Report of the Advisory Commission on Rakhine State:

The Kofi Annan Foundation and the Office of the State Counsellor established an Advisory Commission on Rakhine State in September 2016 in response to a request from Daw Aung San Suu Kyi, Myanmar's State Counsellor. The Commission is a national body, with Myanmarians making up the bulk of its members. It was tasked with looking into the various problems that Rakhine State is facing and coming up with solutions.

In Rakhine State, advisory Member visited with political leaders and communities, as well as government ministers and officials in Naypyitaw, civil society and religious leaders, Myanmar's foreign and regional allies, and individual experts. The attacks on security officers in northern Rakhine State in October 2016 highlighted ,While those attacks and the subsequent security operations heightened tensions, they also strengthened long-term solutions to the insecurity and instability that continue to mar Rakhine State's prospects.

The Commission produced a set of interim recommendations in March 2017, and the government's first moves toward implementing these recommendations. However, as the

Commission's final report shows, there is still a long way to go before we can be confident that Rakhine State's peace and development are secure.

3.2.8 Myanmar's Rohingya Crisis Has Moved into a New and Dangerous Phase By International Crisis Group(2018):

This article looks at the events leading up to the ARSA assaults on August 25, 2017, exposing fresh and critical information regarding the group's planning and the attacks themselves. This is based on interviews with ARSA members, analysis of WhatsApp messages sent by the group and its sympathisers, publicly-posted films, and interviews with villagers in Rakhine State and recently-arrived refugees in Bangladesh conducted in Myanmar and Bangladesh since October 2016. A large portion of the research was carried out by Rohingya-speaking experts. The impact of the crisis on Myanmar is also considered in the paper. Finally, several international policy responses are discussed.

3.2.9 UN Security Council, Report of the Secretary-General on conflict-related sexual violence on Rohingya (23 March 2018):

The current report, which covers the months of January to December 2018, is submitted in accordance with Security Council resolution 2106 (2013), which requests that Commitee report annually on the implementation of Security Council resolution 1960 (2010), as well as make strategic recommendations. The mission and Office of Special Representative on Sexual Violence in Conflict were established ten years ago this year. There has been a paradigm shift in the awareness of the plague of conflict-related sexual assault and its influence on international peace and security, as well as the reaction required to prevent such crimes and the comprehensive services required by survivors, over the last decade.

While the UN is increasingly addressing the problem of sexual violence in conflict from an operational or technical standpoint by strengthening security and justice institutions, it is still critical to recognise and address gender inequality as the root cause and driver of sexual violence, both in war and peace.

3.2.10 Women and Girls Critically Underserved in the Rohingya Humanitarian Response (2018):

According to the Inter-Sector Coordination Group's rapid needs assessment, 60 percent of new arrivals are women and girls, with a significant percentage of pregnant (3%) and breastfeeding mothers (7 percent). This inflow has necessitated a rapid expansion of health and protection services to assist an already vulnerable population fleeing horrible human rights violations. The Bangladesh government, in collaboration with foreign partners, is providing temporary shelter for Rohingya refugees, but it faces an uphill battle in dealing with the crisis' huge scope. To satisfy the sexual and reproductive health (SRH) requirements of women and girls, the response must be strengthened immediately and services expanded. This includes psychosocial clinical, , and other support for sexual violence survivors, as well as unrestricted access to basic sexual and reproductive health care, such as a menstrual regulation, menstrual regulation,full range of contraception methods, menstrual regulation, safe delivery, and emergency obstetric and newborn care for those who require it.

3.3 <u>REVIEW OF ARTICLES:</u>

3.3.1 The Rohingya Refugee Crisis by Rey Ty:

The focus of this article is on a case study of militant Buddhists in Myanmar who violate the rights of entire civilian populations of various religions. The purpose is to analyse the Rohingya refugee situation and to challenge the widespread perception of all Buddhists as proponents of unconditional peace. The text starts with an overview of the historical and current conditions that led to the Rohingya crisis, followed by a consideration of the problem's causes and repercussions. It finishes by proposing a potential agenda for resolving the Rohingya refugee situation.

3.3.2 India needs a refugee and asylum law by The Hindu(Passing Reference):

A long-term refugee policy is essential for managing population migrations rationally and ensuring openness and predictability in our administrative actions. India's leading role in the area and among emerging countries would be reflected in a national refugee management law.

The Act will define the functions of various government, judicial, and UN institutions involved in refugee assistance, as well as the mechanisms for coordination among them. It would also assist to reduce tensions between the host and the origin countries. Other countries would see the decision to provide asylum as a peaceful, humanitarian, and legitimate act, rather than an arbitrary political ploy. Some governments support refugees at first, but then expect them to fend for themselves. A few countries have handled refugees as if they were wards of the state. A national refugee legislation can assist in striking the correct balance between the two.

3.3.3 Passing reference-Rohingya crisis: India sends relief material to Myanmar's Rakhine State Published By Business Standard(25/11/2017):

India has insisted that the situation be handled humanely, that development initiatives be launched in Rakhine, and that conditions be made for the refugees' safe and peaceful return to their homes. Prime Minister Narendra Modi expressed India's worries about the matter during a meeting with Myanmar's State Counsellor Aung San Suu Kyi in September.

3.3.4 The refugee settlements of Kutupalong and Balukhali in Cox's Bazar, Bangladesh, a health survey was conducted by Medicins and Frontiers(2018):

In Kutupalong Makeshift Settlement (KMS), Balukhali Makeshift Settlement (BMS), Kutupalong Makeshift Settlement Extension (KMS Extension), and Balukhali Makeshift Settlement Extension (BMS Extension), four health surveys were conducted (BMS Extension). These locations were chosen to ensure that the health status and conditions of both new and existing settlements were assessed. Current and retrospective mortality, the most common morbidities impacting the population, global and severe acute malnutrition rates, vaccine coverage rates for important antigens, and health-seeking behaviour were all measured in the surveys. A simple random sampling method was employed.

3.3.5 What you need to know about the Rohingya situation in Myanmar By BBC(2020):

Hundreds of thousands of Rohingya Muslims fled to Bangladesh when Myanmar's army launched a brutal campaign on them in August 2017. They risked everything to flee by ship or on foot from a military onslaught later condemned as a "classic example of ethnic cleansing" by the United Nations.

The UN's top court ordered the Buddhist-majority government to take steps to protect its Rohingya people from genocide in January 2020. However, the Myanmar (previously Burma) army has stated that it is fighting Rohingya insurgents and that it is not targeting civilians. Aung San Suu Kyi, the country's leader and a former human rights champion, has frequently dismissed charges of genocide.

3.3.6 BBC, The Rohingya children trafficked for sex. 20 March 2018:

A BBC team travelled to Bangladesh with the Foundation Sentinel, a non-profit organisation dedicated to training and assisting law enforcement agencies combating child exploitation, to investigate the networks behind the trade we'd heard so much about.

3.3.7 The Supreme Court should reconsider its decision to deport Rohingya refugees by Indian Express(Apr 2021)- Passing Reference:

Court should also look at the other concern so other dimension is also important because it is the concern of the human right violation, the damage is not irrevocable because the order in question is an interim order that was issued without a full hearing. As a result, the Court could quickly hear the main petition and clarify the law on non-refoulement and Article 21. By doing so, the Court will gain back its well-deserved image as the "final refuge of the oppressed and befuddled."

3.3.7 In India, Rohingya refugees create a comic book to tell their tales By Indian Express(2020)- Passing Reference:

"A comic book can help us reach out to individuals who are literate as well as those who are illiterate," says Ali Johar, who was only 10 years old when he was forced to quit Myanmar for Bangladesh in 2005. His family relocated to Delhi seven years later. "It's been a never-ending battle," he says. Johar and his family had been living in a shanty in Kalindi Kunj with several other refugees until recently. Despite the fact that he has now relocated to Zakir Nagar, he continues to see his buddies. He is here to promote how he believes that good education is probably the only means for a better tomorrow by managing education scholarships for select youngsters from the community. "My father was a businessman with political ties in Myanmar, but we are refugees in India with no rights; we can't buy property or work for the government." "However, no one can refuse us education," Johar argues. Born Ali-en, a political science graduate student's comic strip, promotes the same concept.

3.3.8 'Kill All You See,' Myanmar Soldiers Tell of Rohingya Slaughter for the First Time By New York Times(2021):

Executions, mass burials, village obliterations, and rape are among the acts confessed by the two soldiers in a monotone, with only a few blinks of the eye revealing emotion. In video evidence, Pvt. Myo Win Tun stated that his superior officer's instruction from August 2017 was unambiguous. "Shoot whatever you see and hear."

He claimed he followed orders and took part in the slaughter of 30 Rohingya Muslims, who were buried in a mass grave near a cell tower and a military post.

3.3.9 How the Rohingya Escaped By New York Times:

Soldiers shot, raped, and set fire to the homes of almost two-thirds of Myanmar's Rohingya Muslim population this year. It's one of the fastest mass exoduses in human history. The New York Times dispatched several correspondents to the area to report on the situation.

3.3.10 Crimes against Rohingyas: ICC prosecutor calls for collaboration to bring justice to the Rohingyas: by Dhaka Tribune(2022):

Karim AA Khan QC, the Prosecutor of the International Criminal Court (ICC), has stressed the importance of collective accountability in moving beyond talking about justice to actually delivering it for the Rohingyas.

3.4 REVIEW OF DOCUMENTARY:
3.4.1 Myanmar's Killing Fields:

Myanmar's hope was Nobel Laureate Aung San Suu Kyi. She's now being accused of standing by while the military mounted a horrific campaign against Rohingya Muslims in Myanmar. FRONTLINE investigates hidden recordings and speaks with victims of a campaign labelled by the UN as having "all the characteristics of genocide."

The Myanmar military's deadly onslaught against the Rohingyas was secretly recorded on video. Children between the ages of five and six have their throats cut. Children are tossed into fires. Women and children are being raped in large numbers. Entire villages were destroyed by fire.

Myanmar's Killing Fields is the most extensive examination to date of Myanmar security forces' systematic massacre of Rohingya Muslims, an action recognised by the United Nations as having "all the markings of genocide." The video depicts a people's intended destruction and uncovers new proof that security personnel committed crimes against humanity. Never-before-seen footage shot by a hidden network of citizen activists, firsthand testimonials from victims and their families, and candid observations from top dignitaries who claim to have questioned Aung San Suu Kyi about the issue are included. For years, Muslim Rohingyas have lived in Myanmar's Rakhine State, but the government regards many of them as illegal immigrants from Bangladesh. Myanmar's Killing Fields reveals the storey of a planned campaign against Rohingya Muslims in majority-Buddhist Myanmar dating back more than 5 years — long before their escape became global news — with disturbing footage filmed by the covert activist network.

The filmmakers spent six months interviewing dozens of witnesses, comparing their testimonies, and cross-checking them with human rights investigators in order to independently confirm the footage and other videos. The data refutes Myanmar's military's claim that their bloodshed was only a counter-insurgency "clearing operation" against ARSA, a militant Islamic Rohingya group that had attacked and killed security forces at police and army bases. "These were not isolated incidents. Former UN High Commissioner Zeid al Hussein tells

FRONTLINE that the meetings were "well-organized and well-thought-out." "There's a pattern to this... This was an example of ethnic cleansing in its purest form." Victims of severe brutality relate their stories in Myanmar's Killing Fields: Mumtaz Begum, who survived a slaughter at Tula Toli, recalls, "My five-year-old was tossed into the river." "I was carrying a two-year-old child on my hip." They snatched the infant from his mother and hurled him into the fire... My kid was wailing as they raped me, so they macheted her three times.

Chapter 4

STUDY OF POST DISPLACEMENT TRAUMA

This research examines the factors that contribute to mental health issues among Rohingya refugees and asylum seekers in India, as well as the challenges that care providers face. As a result, it draws attention to a variety of interventions that are needed to help Rohingya refugees deal with mental health issues. This includes the MHFSS framework's holistic framework of action, which includes pharmacotherapy, psychological interventions, and psychosocial support, as well as policy advocacy and cultural competency capacity building for agencies working with the Rohingya in order to develop long-term solutions. Overall, more research is needed to fill the information void that currently exists.

4.1 Rohingya refugees In India:

Following continuous persecution by Myanmar's military and police, Rohingyas have sought shelter in Bangladesh, India, Indonesia, Malaysia, and other neighboring countries. Rohingyas take help agents to cross international borders. They have departed their homeland, leaving behind everything of their possessions.

During the data collection procedure, I discovered the following:

The refugee would enlist the assistance of dealers to reach India. They'd assemble a group, cross the Myanmar-India border, and enter Indian territory (around Kolkata) without being detected. They would halt in Kolkata after entering Indian soil before departing by train to destinations such as Jammu and Kashmir, Delhi, Uttar Pradesh, Mumbai, Hyderabad etc.

(a) Housing temporarily and precarious living conditions: Since 2012, and even before that, the Rohingya have been displaced for an extended period of time. The humanitarian aid provided by the UNHCR is insufficient to address the needs for decent living circumstances, development, and long-term livelihoods. However, the main issue is that the Rohingya are unregistered refugees in India. In India, the bulk of Rohingya refugee families reside in temporary settlements, which are clusters of refugee houses living in close houses/huts. Private owners or landlords own and control the land where housing sheds are built or dwellings are rented. A small group of Rohingya people live on land granted for charity purposes by the Humanitarian Trust organisation in New Delhi. The Rohingya, like other urban refugees, live in rented homes in urban settlements or in residential and commercial centres in New Delhi.

(b) As a result, Rohingya refugees in Delhi and the surrounding cities face a significant problem with shelter security. They will be denied refuge easily because to their precarious legal status under international law, particularly as a result of their illegal infiltration and trespassing into Indian territory. Furthermore, due to lengthy bilateral discussions, they may be forced to live in makeshift shelter sheds. The majority of Rohingya prefer to live in cluster settlements because they have easier access to humanitarian aid in the form of charity donations from local and international humanitarian organizations. In all settlements, the lack of a safe and secure water supply is a key concern. There are no pakka toilets available to any of the families. They use shared sanitation of one or two or possibly all of the families living together as a sanitation facility. Though the UNHCR card provides them with some protection from incarceration in India, it is unable to provide them with complete access to education, health services, and a means of subsistence unless and until volunteers in certain clinics and schools intervene. Refugees, on the other hand, have the right to free education and health treatment as a result of UNHCR's efforts to mediate these services so that they can reach them.

(c) Living in Delhi has a number of socio-economic concerns: The lack of proper measures to assist refugees in finding suitable living places has resulted in the form of socio-economic issues that they face. It is tough to supply housing space in Delhi due to the large number of people migrating to the city. As fault lines emerge, evacuees will be forced to seek safety in the city's underbelly. In this way, the UNHCR fails to fulfil its responsibility to safeguard refugees. However, existing fault lines reveal that refugee mobility is tied to the possibility of finding work and making a livelihood. The difficulties arise mostly because Rohingyas are unable to diversify or pursue career opportunities in the city due to their non-recognition. They are fundamentally and significantly relegated to working in the informal sector, which is where they live.

(d) Forms of job and difficulties in finding acceptable work: The majority of Rohingyas in India work for daily pay in the informal economy. The revenues are hardly enough to keep the families afloat. The Rohingya are responsible for rubbish collection. They travel to collect trash from the surrounding areas. At the rubbish pickup station, single women sort the garbage. They are compelled to conduct this filthy task where they live.

The second most common job among Rohingya is driving an auto-rickshaw. They can only drive short distances around their enclave or community up to the main intersection and between the metro station and their enclave, therefore this has limits.

(e) Refugee life: Human Security, Migration, Family Needs, and Psychosocial Aspects: Due to migration to various countries in South and Southeast Asia, the Rohingya refugees confront a major problem of family separation. The second issue is in-country migration. They are separated from their kin and family, who are scattered across Bangladesh in camps. Some members of the family are asylum seekers in Malaysia. Susceptibility to trafficking and exploitation, early marriage for girls, gender-based violence in places where they live, violence against children, rape and abuse of refugee girls in asylum countries, and the impact of the living environment on the health and psycho-social well-being of refugee children are just a few of the many protection challenges that Rohingya refugees face. These are also the source of many of the security issues that refugees face.

4.2 <u>General health aspects:</u>

Rakhine State has less developed healthcare than the other states in Myanmar. Because of their statelessness and significant limitations on their mobility, Rohingya have a difficult time accessing and using health care. Because they cannot pursue university education in Myanmar, government and non-governmental health facilities in Rakhine State are Operated by a national medical staff of other ethnicities. Poor health outcomes among Rohingya refugees may be due to limited access to formal health services, such as public hospitals and government clinics, due to long-standing prejudice and travel restrictions. Traditional healers, herbalists, shopkeepers (who provide medicines and medical advice), and faith or religious healers are often sought out by Rohingyas seeking alternative conventional practices such as homemade medicinal remedies or seeking advice from traditional healers, herbalists, shopkeepers (who provide medicines and medical advice), and faith or religious healers.[22]

---

[22] Constantine, G (2012), *Exiled to Nowhere: Burma's Rohingya*, Nowhere People, Wagenbach Verlag

Nutrition:

The most vulnerable groups in need of nutritional care are infants, children under the age of five, pregnant and breastfeeding women, and adolescent girls. Prior to the 2017 unrest, the prevalence of Global Acute Malnutrition (GAM) and Severe Acute Malnutrition (SAM) in Rakhine State had already exceeded the WHO Crisis Classification's emergency nutrition limits. From May to October 2017, a Nutrition Assessment in one of Cox's Bazar's refugee communities revealed that GAM was prevalent at 24.3 percent, while SAM, a strong predictor of mortality in children under the age of five, had doubled to 7.5 percent.[23] Although the prevalence of acute malnutrition is decreasing, according to the results of the most recent round of nutrition assessments in the camps in May 2018, it remains unacceptably high, with many aggravating factors such as a high disease burden, and poor WASH, shelter environment, and the rainy season. [24] Stunting, or chronic malnutrition, which is a measure of longer-term nutritional deficits, is high at about 40%, and anemia, which is regarded as a proxy for a micronutrient-poor diet, is also high at over 30% – however, there has been a decrease since October 2017.[25]

Infant and young child feeding practices among Rohingya refugees in Bangladesh are poor, with low rates of exclusive breastfeeding and delayed nursing beginning among infants under six months old. This could be linked to a prevalent practice in Myanmar and Bangladesh of feeding a sweet beverage (sweetened with sugar or honey) to a newborn shortly after birth. This practice was reported by over 70% of caregivers in a May 2018 survey. Minimum acceptable diet is a dietary diversity and meal frequency indicator for children aged 6 to 23 months, and it has been demonstrated to be especially inadequate in this demographic, with 7.3 percent of children in the makeshift camps falling into this category. In the second half of 2018, an in-depth Infant and Young Child Feeding (IYCF) evaluation is planned to delve deeper into the practises in order to better adapt interventions for the prevention of malnutrition in young children. According to the Rupali 7 Families with a malnourished child (ganda) may be hesitant

---

[23] World Food Programme (2011), *Food Security Assessment in the Northern part of Rakhine State,* Rome(Italy)
https://documents.wfp.org/stellent/groups/public/documents/ena/wfp234781.pdf
[24] WHO(2009), *Child growth criteria and the detection of severe acute malnutrition in new-borns and children: a joint statement,* World Health Organization. Geneva,
http://apps.who.int/iris/bitstream/handle/10665/44129/9789241598163_eng.pdf;jsessionid=C45DC43487FEEC
FB9DC7A1982F7EAE3D?sequence=1
[25] Nutrition Sector(2018), Emergency Nutrition Assessment: Preliminary Results (April 28 – May 28, Nutrition Sector: Cox's Bazar, Bangladesh,
https://www.humanitarianresponse.info/sites/www.humanitarianresponse.info/files/assessments/180612_emerge
ncy_nutrition_assessment_round_2_ms_nyp_preliminary_results.pdf

to seek aid out of shame, fearing that doing so will reveal that the family has failed to care for the youngster.[26]

4.3 Mental Health Of Rohingya Refugees:

Mental health is an essential part of public health, as it affects one's quality of life and ability to cope with life's ups and downs. Physical illness, social inequity, and an unhealthy lifestyle are all protected by mental health.

Individuals' mental health is negatively impacted by difficult living conditions and stressful life events, which is why refugees, asylum seekers, and migrants are among the most vulnerable groups in terms of mental health. On the one hand, difficult living conditions and potentially traumatic events in the country of origin; on the other hand, the process of leaving the country and the difficulties people face during their journey, as well as challenges of adaptation and establishing a new life in the country of destination, present several mental health challenges.

When I was conducting interview one of the interviews Faarq, a Rohingya refugee who arrived in India in 2012, said, "I haven't heard from my family members in 5 years." "My brother told me the last time we spoke on the phone that several military soldiers had taken down our house's fence." Now since they haven't phoned or returned my calls in such a long time, I'm concerned that something is amiss." So Faarq is try to convey his feeling, we are not safe in Myanmar, Militaries are doing a lot of atrocity in the Rakhine region that leads to mental trauma.

Another Interviews Aadeel came to India in 2012 after leaving Myanmar. He works at a Fashion Point as a security guard. He explained that he gets paid in daily wages rather than a regular income He also explained 'we all very fearful due to such atrocity.

The Rohingya mental health crisis is life-threatening and has largely gone unnoticed. The scope of the problem is enormous, but it is not insurmountable. Governments should place a high priority on the mental health of the Rohingya population, ensuring that survivors of Myanmar's genocide may rebuild their lives in dignity. Reliving traumatic incidents was one of the most commonly reported symptoms among Rohingya refugees in India. More than 60% of Rohingyas, for example, reported having "recurrent thoughts or memories of the most upsetting

---

[26] Ripoli, S.(2017), *Within a humanitarian setting, social and cultural issues influence the Rohingya's health, nutrition, well-being, and protection*, UNICEF, https://opendocs.ids.ac.uk/opendocs/handle/20.500.12413/13328

or horrifying occurrence," "feeling as if the event is occurring again," and "recurrent nightmares." The majority of Rohingya people are suffering from Post-Traumatic Stress Disorder, a significant mental health disorder that can make it difficult to live a productive life.

"I envision what the military and Buddhists have done to me while I attempt to sleep," a 35-year-old Rohingya ladies shared with the research. "I have the impression that they are approaching, pursuing, and shooting at me." I recall how they hacked and slaughtered individuals, as well as throwing children into fires. When I'm in bed, the pain of the Reality and Trauma comes to my mind."

4.4 Epidemiological studies of mental disorders and risk/protective factors:

While I found a large amount of mental health research among Myanmar's ethnic groupings, there are few published papers that particularly address the mental health and psychosocial situation of Rohingya people. In my literature study, I found six publications with broad implications for this group's mental health and psychological well-being. Qualitative research conducted in India in 2022 revealed a significant level of mistrust among Rohingya refugees, as well as a fear of exploitation by fellow Rohingya. Based on these research, the estimated prevalence of mental health issues and related protective/risk factors are shown in the table below. There were no comprehensive epidemiological studies of Rohingya in my research. Taken together, the studies show a high incidence of a variety of mental health issues, including the endorsement of symptoms linked with Posttraumatic Stress Disorder (PTSD) and depression. Other mental health difficulties, such as explosive rage, psychotic-like symptoms, somatic or medically unexplained symptoms, reduced functioning, and suicidal ideation, are also frequently reported. Because the metrics have not been validated for the Rohingya population, caution should be given in interpreting these findings.[27]

Psychiatric epidemiology studies undertaken with war-affected communities have revealed considerable variances in the frequency of mental diseases. These differences could be due to contextual factors, methodological difficulties, the use of various instruments, or the passage of time after a dispute. When using typical self-report surveys, there is a particularly high danger of transcultural measurement error. Future research is needed to look at the nature and

---

[27] Charlson, F.J, *Post-traumatic stress disorder and major depression in conflict-affected populations: an epidemiological model and predictor analysis*. Global Mental Health (Camb), 2016, https://www.ncbi.nlm.nih.gov/pmc/articles/PMC5314754/

progression of symptoms; for example, they could be normal and not impede with adaptation, or they could become maladaptive/pathological over time.[28]

Table- Description of current stressors and MHPSS related distress among Rohingya refugees in Delhi(India) in February 2022

Group	Current Stressors (In Delhi)	Sign of MHPSS distress and Issues
Children	No educational facility, Lack of space, dysfunctional family environment, lack of toys, lack of care	Crying, irritation, low mood, aggressive Behaviour
Adolescents (boys)	No playground, Lack of freedom in movement, lack of clothing, limited or no educational facilities, poor relations among siblings, difficulties in making friends, safety and security tension and poor socio-economic situation,	Poor appetite, Excessive anger, substance abuse, quarrelling, crying, risky behaviours
Adolescents (girls)	Excessive heat/hot temperature, lack of hygiene products, lack of clothing, poor light and ventilation inside the houses, being married without parents' consent (reported by community), poor bathing conditions, lack of safety and gender based violence	Increased stress and anxiety, Lack of interest in daily activities, crying, isolation, anger, psychosomatic symptoms (such as, sleeping disturbance, lack of appetite), suicidal thought

---

[28] Silove, D. P. Ventevogel, and S. Rees, *The contemporary refugee crisis: an overview of mental health challenges*. World Psychiatry, 2017. 16(2): p. 130–139, https://www.hhri.org/publication/the-contemporary-refugee-crisis-an-overview-of-mental-health-challenges/

Women	Scarcity of water sources, long distance from house to sanitation facilities, insufficient food, inability to properly feed children, lack of freedom, lack of convenient house, fear of being abused at home and outside, long wait times for any services, lack of space for socialising outside of their sheds	Excessive anger, stress, Passing most of the time in the house which results into limited social networking/ support, stress linked to re-productive health related problems, lack of interest in daily activities, expression of anger on children (eg. beating), stress outburst with elderly people, feeling of hopelessness and suffocation, poor relation with husband
Men	Unemployment, lack of activity, having no independent work or workplace, Facing Difficulties to support family	Anxiety, Irritation, worries about family and future, stress related to tension with children and wife/wives, rude behaviour
Elderly People	No free space for elderly people, lack of proper clothing, hot temperature, tension due to lack of burial facilities, lack of treatment facilities, food insecurity, having no prayer room	Feeling of suffocation, Irritation, laziness, poor communication, crying, shouting, low mood, anxiety about their funerals, rumination of distressful or traumatic experiences, emotional numbness
Person with disabilities	No activity, Poor living conditions, lack of treatment facilities, inability to walk, loneliness, deprivation from basic needs, willingness to be active but lack of facilities for persons with disability	Loneliness, Irritation, odd behaviour, sadness, no work, anxiety, crying, not being able to communicate with family members properly

4.5 <u>Role of the health sector in MHPSS:</u>
Access to general health care:

Rohingya populations in Myanmar continue to face prejudice in healthcare, and they are unable to self-refer to medical treatment centres outside of their allocated dwelling regions.

Due to their statelessness, insufficient legal protection and safeguards, lack of financial means, and the deterrent nature of immigration policies against refugees and asylum seekers in Bangladesh and other neighbouring countries hosting refugees, Rohingya face formidable challenges in accessing appropriate healthcare and mental health services.

Medical care was initially unavailable in the refugee settlements built in India in late 2018. Many organizations and national and international volunteers travelled to Delhi or other parts of India to support the creation of temporary clinics, mobile clinics, and field hospitals to provide health treatment for refugees. Many short-term missions have concluded, but agencies and organizations continued providing health services.

Unemployment's Effects on Mental Health:

Unemployment can be a rollercoaster of emotions. As time passes and no new employment is found, what started as excitement and optimism for a new job might develop into bitterness, sadness, and resentment. The impact of unemployment on mental health can grow more severe and possibly evolve into mental health issues when people are unemployed for long periods of time.

Loss of Focus: One of the many psychological impacts of unemployment is the feeling that you have lost your sense of purpose. Jobs make people feel more productive and like they are contributing members of society, which helps to give their life meaning. Some people may lose their sense of purpose when they lose their work. They will most likely feel useless or empty until they find a new job. These feelings can signify that you're heading down the path to depression.

Depression: Unemployment often leads to depression. The initial impacts of losing a job might leave people unhappy and upset, but as time passes, hopelessness about finding another work can set in, and depression can set in. According to a poll of South-east Asian citizens, people who are unemployed are twice as likely to have participated in a depression treatment program, either previously or currently. This disparity worsens over time, with 19 percent of persons who have been unemployed for 52 weeks or more receiving treatment.

Insecurity: Work may be how some individuals define success, and if they don't have it, they may feel like a failure. This mindset, along with the fact that they are unable to provide basic necessities for their families, can lead to self-doubt and insecurity in some people.

The longer they go without new employment, the more their confidence is shattered.

Anxiety: Another common side effect of unemployment is anxiety. When comparing unemployed males to employed men, anxiety was considerably higher in the unemployed group than in the employed group. With a job loss, it's reasonable to be concerned about money, but these concerns may grow over time, necessitating anxiety disorder treatment.

Irritability: All of the issues mentioned above, along with the aggravation of not being able to locate another employment, can make people irritable and furious. They may become more irritable with their loved ones or become enraged over their previously overlooked minor infractions.

Not everyone can deal with their mental health issues in an effective way, mainly if they are bored at home during the workday. Instead, these people may turn to drugs or alcohol to feel better. This negative behaviour might turn into a substance abuse problem, which can lead to even more issues.

4.6 The connection between mental health and unemployment/low Income:

Unemployment, defined as being out of work and actively looking for work, has been shown to have a detrimental impact on a variety of health outcomes.

Socio-Economic Situation in Rakhine By UNDP:

Myanmar GDP per capita for 2020 was $1,400, Rakhine has a population of over 2.7 million people, with roughly 1.1 million (or 42 percent) living below the national poverty line. An additional one million persons (40 percent of the total population) are in a precarious economic situation. These values are the second highest among Myanmar's states and regions. Nearly 57 percent of Rakhine households' whole monthly income is spent on food. Agriculture is the most common source of work in Myanmar's rural areas (67 percent of total primary jobs), followed by services (20 percent), and industry (13 percent). The same is true in Rakhine, where agricultural activities employ 79 percent of the population.[29]

Unemployment can impair one's health through many mechanisms:

1. as a result of the loss of the day-to-day structure of work or the stigma associated with unemployment, which causes stress and low self-esteem.

2. people are stressed as a result of financial difficulties, insecurity, and diminished future earning potential (which damages health)

3. from the social security system itself, which, through the claims procedure, employment capacity tests, and job search conditions, can have a negative impact on mental health.

The negative effects of unemployment on mental health, life satisfaction, and physical health have risen with time.

Long durations of reduced income, job loss, or unemployment have resulted from pandemic restrictions, and the length of these circumstances is particularly concerning. The policymakers' concern about unemployment, particularly among young people, arises in part from the long-term negative impact that unemployment can have on future earning capacity. However, research suggests that young unemployment (and several periods of unemployment) have long-term mental health consequences.

---

[29]UNDP(2020), *Assessment Of COVID-19 Socio-Economic Impact On Rural Communities In Rakhine* By UNDP,file:///C:/Users/layci/Downloads/undp-mm-Rapidsocio-economicImpactAssessment-COVID-19-Rakhine-nov2020%20(2).pdf

4.7 **Data Analysis:**

	Occupation	Wage For Local	Unit	Wage for Rohingya	Unit
M A N	Daily Labourer	400-700	Rupees/day	250-400	Rupees/day
	Farm Worker	300-500	Rupees/day	200-300	Rupees/day
	Rickshaw puller	250-600	Rupees/day	200-500	Rupees/day
	Tea Stall(Bu..)	5000-15000	Rupees/Month	4000-8000	Rupees/Month
	Domestic work	300-600	Rupees/day	200-400	Rupees/day
	Hotel Cook	300-700	Rupees/day	200-450	Rupees/day
W O M E N	Camp Volunteer	NA	Rupees/day	300-500	Rupees/day
	Cloth Seller	300-1500	Rupees/day	250-1000	Rupees/day
	Other goods seller	200-1000	Rupees/day	200-500	Rupees/day
	Cleaner	300-500	Rupees/day	250-400	Rupees/day

The refugee's main occupations are day labourers, vehicle drivers, Rickshaw pullers, Hotel cooks, Camp volunteers, and a few who are better off owning a modest shop providing daily necessities. In addition, the settlement contains a tiny mosque and a small madrassa where people can pray. They live in a makeshift structure composed of bamboo, wood, ply, and plastic sheets. These houses are in close proximity to one another and lack sufficient ventilation, natural light, electricity, and other amenities. Although the water quality is exceedingly poor and unsafe for human consumption, the residents of this village share shared restrooms and three hand-pumps for water supply. Furthermore, there is a lack of basic sanitation and cleanliness in the neighbourhood.

Low Levels Income:

Poverty raises the risk of mental health issues and can be both a cause and a result of mental illness. The social, economic, and physical surroundings in which people live have many characteristics (including inequities) that influence mental health. Supporting the mental health and well-being of people living in poverty and lowering the number of persons with mental health problems living in poverty necessitates an understanding of this complexity.

The review presents a conceptual framework for understanding the relationship between poverty and mental health that includes a life course analysis, a discussion of the socio-economic factors (or social determinants) that impact mental health and poverty, human rights, equity, anti-stigma, and non-discrimination principles, and prevention, self-management, peer support, community development, and social movement building approaches.

4.8 Towards a multi-layered service and support system:

Following the publication of the IASC Guidelines for Mental Health and Psychosocial Support in Emergency Settings, it has become clear that MHPSS services should be viewed as a multi-layered system of services and supports. Professionals working in (mental) health services (particularly specialists with advanced mental health training) and those who start and strengthen community-based psychosocial activities will be affected by this. MHPSS services and assistance are not limited to a small group of experts but must be integrated into current sectors such as health, security, and education.

Layer 1: Consideration of social factors in basic services and security:

Ensure that basic needs and essential services (food, shelter, water, sanitation, basic health care, communicable disease control) and security are provided in ways that respect the dignity of all people, taking gender mainstreaming approaches into account, and are inclusive of those with special vulnerabilities, while also avoiding exclusively targeting a single group to minimize tension among beneficiaries and preventing exploitation.[30]

---

[30] Charlson, F.J, *Post-traumatic stress disorder and major depression in conflict-affected populations: an epidemiological model and predictor analysis.* Global Mental Health (Camb), 2016. 3: p. e4.

Strengthening community and family support is the **second layer**. Support the re-establishment or growth of refugee community-based structures that are representative of the population in terms of age, gender, and diversity, as well as other activities that create social cohesion among refugee populations. This includes the promotion of community systems and family support, which use participatory techniques to protect and support members.

Child-Friendly Spaces, community self-help organizations, and establishing networks of refugee volunteers that provide psychosocial and practical support to other refugees are examples of this sort of intervention.

Focused psychosocial support is the **third layer**. Provide emotional and practical help to persons who are having problems coping through individual, family, or group interventions, relying only on their personal strengths and current support network. Following training and continuing supervision, non-specialized personnel in health, education, child protection, or community services typically deliver such interventions. Problem Management Plus Group Interpersonal Therapy for Depression and Integrated ADAPT Therapy are two examples of manualized scalable psychological interventions.[31]

Clinical services (layer 4):

Deliver and ensure that persons with severe symptoms or a level of suffering that has rendered them unable to carry out fundamental daily duties have fair and equitable access to clinical mental health care. Those with pre-existing mental health illnesses and emergency-related difficulties, such as psychosis, drug misuse, severe depression, crippling anxiety symptoms, severe posttraumatic stress symptoms, and those who are in danger of harming themselves or others, frequently make up this group. These interventions are normally led by mental health experts, however, many tasks can be completed by other health professionals (doctors and nurses) if they are thoroughly trained and supervised in the use of the mhGAP materials.

The significant emotional anguish and continuous systematic discrimination faced by Rohingya refugees present great hurdles, and humanitarian workers can easily get overwhelmed in the face of multiple demands. The current crisis, on the other hand, brings with it fresh resources and opportunities for developing culturally relevant and contextually

---

[31] Silove, D., P. Ventevogel, and S. Rees(2017), *The contemporary refugee crisis: an overview of mental health challenges,* World Psychiatry, 2017. 16(2): p. 130–139.

suitable services and supports. Past trauma exposure and losses must be balanced with present pressures and concerns about the future. MHPSS interventions should be designed in such a way that they activate and build on refugees' individual and collective strengths. MHPSS employees must work alongside Rohingya refugees rather than just for them in order to achieve this. It's critical to have a good knowledge of how Rohingya people think about their problems and seek solutions. [32] In an emergency, the IASC provides extensive guidelines that aids humanitarian actors in planning, establishing, and coordinating basic multi-sectoral responses to safeguard and improve mental health and psychosocial well-being.

---

[32] Human Rights Watch, *All of my body was pain: Sexual violence against Rohingya women and girls in Burma.* 2017,USA.

CHAPTER- 5

Conclusion And Way forward

Outsiders see the Rohingya as one of the world's most mistreated ethnic and religious minority, but many Myanmar resumes see them as a rebellious foreign group. Myanmar's democratic system is faulty because no one or institution appears to be in charge of making a clear declaration and implementing a clear policy action based on the rule of law and without prejudice. "The most effective way to kill people is to deny and annihilate their own understanding of their past," George Orwell says.[33]

The attacks on the Rohingya civilian population are in violation of international human rights and humanitarian law, often known as war laws. Crimes against peace, crimes against humanity, and war crimes are among the crimes committed. "The Rohingya are one of the most vulnerable people on the planet," said UN Secretary General Ban Ki-moon.

5.1 The scenario of Refugee in India:

A brief examination of the refugee issue in India will assist put the intricacies of law enforcement in a number of situations affecting refugees into correct perspective. For millennia, India has been a refugee haven. From the period when practically the entire Zoroastrian population fled to India to escape persecution on religious grounds in Iran, India has continued to welcome huge numbers of refugees from other countries, not just from the bordering countries. The most important point to note is that there has never been a single instance of a refugee originating from Indian land, with the exception of the transboundary movement of people during the 1947 split of the country. On the other hand, it has always been a welcoming country, expanding its multi-cultural and multi-ethnic fabric in the process. India has welcomed refugees from all religions and groups, in keeping with its secular policy. It is important to note that India has welcomed refugees not just from its neighbours but also from far-flung countries such as Afghanistan, Iran, Iraq, Somalia, Sudan, and Uganda since its independence.[34]

---

[33] Shanker, R., & Vijayaraghavan, H. (2020, November), *Refugee recognition challenges in India,* FMR online, https://www.fmreview.org/recognising-refugees/shanker-vijayaraghavan

[34] India firm on deporting Rohingya. Retrieved from The Hindu: https://www.thehindu.com/news/national/other-states/india-firm-on-deportingrohingya/article19625028

Refugees from one or more neighbouring countries have frequently crossed the border into India in the South Asian subcontinent. Given the sensitivity of national and regional politics in the subcontinent, the issue of refugees entering into India cannot be separated from the broader security challenges that affect the region. India had well over 2,10,541 refugees at the end of 30th June 2021(UNCR Fact Sheet), not including those from Afghanistan, Iran, Iraq, Somalia, Sudan, and Uganda.

5.2 <u>The Indian Legal Framework and Refugees:</u>

The Indian legal system confronts refugees on two levels. There are regulations that govern their entry into and stay in India, as well as a slew of other difficulties. There are a number of constitutional and legal rules that refugees may be concerned about depending on their situation.

5.3 <u>Provisions of the Constitution</u>

A few articles of the Indian Constitution apply to refugees on Indian soil in the same way that they apply to Indian citizens.

The Indian Supreme court has consistently held that Article 21 of the Indian Constitution guarantees the Fundamental Right to Personal Liberty and Life to all citizens and non - citizens alike. The Indian High Courts have liberally applied natural justice concepts to refugee cases, while also recognised the United Nation's High Commissioner for Refugees (UNHCR) as a key participant in refugee protection. In a series of judgements, the Hon'ble High Court of Guwahati has acknowledged the refugee issue, allowing refugees to petition to the UNHCR for a determination of asylum status while deportation orders issued by the district court or the administration are stayed. Furthermore, India's Constitution supports international law respect under Article 51(c). In the cases of Gurunathan and others vs. Government of India and others and A.C.Mohd.Siddique vs. Government of India and others, the Madras High Court expressed its unwillingness to allow any Sri Lankan refugees to be forced to return to their homeland against their will. "There is no question of deporting the Iranian refugee to Iran, since he has been recognised as a refugee by the UNHCR," the Bombay High Court said in Syed Ata

Mohammadi vs. Union of India. The Hon'ble Court also permitted the refugee to travel to any country he desired. This order adheres to internationally agreed-upon standards of "non-refoulement" of refugees to their home countries.

The Supreme Court ruled in NHRC vs Arunachal Pradesh that the state is obligated to defend the life and liberty of every human being, citizen or not. Even though, India is unwilling to accept and assist Rohingya refugees. The importance of voluntary nature of repatriation was emphasised in P. Nedumaran vs. Union of India, and the Court held that the UNHCR, as a global agency, was to ascertain the voluntariness of the refugees, and that it was not for the Court to consider whether consent was voluntary. In cases like Maiwand's Trust of Afghan Human Freedom vs. State of Punjab and N.D.Pancholi vs. State of Punjab & Others, the Supreme Court of India has halted deportation of refugees. In Malavika Karlekar vs. Union of India, the Supreme Court ordered the deportation of Andaman Island Burmese refugees to be stayed because "their claim for refugee status was pending adjudication and a prima facie case for grant of refugee status is made out." The Supreme Court's ruling in the Chakma refugee case stated unequivocally that no one's life or liberty can be taken away without due process of law. The Supreme Court has already stressed the same argument in the cases of Luis De Raedt vs. Union of India and State of Arunachal Pradesh vs. KhudiramChakma.

5.4 **The International Community's Position on the Rohingya Crisis and its Impact on Neighboring Countries:**

Thailand, Bangladesh, Malaysia, Indonesia, and other Southeast Asian countries have been disproportionately affected by the Rohingya crisis, which has had a social and economic impact on these countries. There is a large influx of Rohingya Muslims into these countries, and they have no say in the matter, as they are not given the option of accepting or rejecting such massive human invasion. Each of these countries has taken in Rohingya refugees, willingly or unwillingly. These countries have also taken steps to halt Rohingya Muslim migration and have attempted to draw international attention to the problem. They have also been unwilling to allow Rohingya Muslims into their countries, seeking to discourage or actively prohibit them from entering. Many Rohingya people opt to cross the border into Bangladesh from Rakhine state, where they live in conditions similar to those they left behind in Myanmar. Around 30,000 Rohingya people dwell in Bangladesh's recognised camps, where they can receive aid from the UN and other humanitarian organisations. At least 200,000 Rohingya people live in unauthorised camps or surrounding villages, receiving no aid and facing deportation to

Myanmar at any time. Bangladesh has also become a secondary point of departure for Rohingya, from which they can travel to other countries in the region by boat.[35]

"We have treated [migrants] with humanity, but they cannot continue to flood our beaches in this manner... "They're not welcome here," says the narrator.

Wan JunaidiJafaar, Malaysian Deputy Home Minister

Thailand, along with Bangladesh, is one of the countries that has played a particularly major role in the Rohingya crisis. Thailand has been the site of multiple violations against the Rohingya and others as a global hub for human trafficking. People from the Rohingya minority are smuggled into Thailand before being trafficked to other countries. A recent crackdown in the country on people trafficking and smuggling has actually aggravated the situation. Smugglers were afraid of being apprehended by the Thai government, so they began leaving boats full of Rohingya refugees in the ocean or on nearby islands. The majority were left without basic necessities such as food or water. Thai officials have also been accused of collaborating with smugglers and ignoring "transit camps" on the Thai-Malaysian border. Smugglers run these camps, where migrants are forced to live in appalling conditions until their families agree to pay a payment. In Thailand, hidden tombs have lately been discovered in abandoned transit camps.[36]

ASEAN, a regional association of 10 Southeast Asian countries, has expressed concern over the Rohingya situation but has done nothing to urge Myanmar to make improvements. This lack of action has been cited by critics as proof of ASEAN's general ineffectiveness. However, as the crisis worsens and ASEAN member states struggle to cope with the influx of refugees, they may be pushed to take more concrete steps in support of the Rohingya. Because the Rohingya migrant issue grew so dramatically in 2017 and 2015, the international community began putting pressure on neighbouring countries to be more humanitarian and proactive in their treatment of the Rohingya.[37]

---

[35] Baker, R. (2010), *Customary International Law in the 21st Century: Old Challenges and New Debates*, European Journal of International Law, Volume 21, Issue 1, February 2010, Pages 173–204, https://doi.org/10.1093/ejil/chq015

[36] Amnesty International(2016) *"We are at breaking point,"& "Rohingya: oppressed in Myanmar, neglected in Bangladesh."*, https://www.amnesty.org/en/documents/asa16/5362/2016/en/

[37] Prasse-Freeman, E(2017), The Rohingya Crisis, Anthropology Today, https://doi.org/10.1111/1467-8322.12389

Indonesia and Malaysia have begun to provide migrants with temporary refuge. Malaysia started rescuing stranded migrant boats. Thailand pledged to refrain from dragging migrant boats into international waters. Myanmar's navy has even started rescuing people. While these measures are a positive start in dealing with the Rohingya problem, more has to be done both in Myanmar and in surrounding countries to protect the Rohingya's lives and rights. Taking a Stand – There is pressure on India, the region's dominating power and a country with a long tradition of providing humanitarian help to its neighbours, to take some measures toward the problem, both domestically and internationally. India has significant clout in both Myanmar and Bangladesh, and it has the potential to make a significant difference. India, on the other hand, has not been perceived to raise the subject of human rights violations. In addition, rather of being sympathetic or sympathetic to the plight of the Rohingya, India's government has characterised them as illegal migrants who must be deported. The Indian Ministry of Home Affairs has issued directives to concerned states to identify and return illegal Rohingya to Myanmar. In addition, the government has filed a lawsuit with the Indian Supreme Court, claiming that the Rohingya are both illegal migrants and a national security concern. When the crisis erupted, with hundreds of fleeing refugees dying in dangerous conditions, New Delhi's firm stance was chastised by the international community, including the UN High Commissioner for Human Rights. The biggest shock came in September, when India's prime minister paid a visit to Myanmar. "We are partners in your concerns over the loss of lives of security officers and innocent people due to extremist violence in Rakhine State," Modi said at a joint press conference with Suu Kyi. Modi not only avoided mentioning the term Rohingya, probably at the request of his host, but he also failed to address the state's persecution and continuous displacement of the Rohingya. In short, New Delhi's attitude appears to be motivated by a cold cost-benefit analysis of commerce with Myanmar, preserving leverage over China, and continuing counterinsurgency cooperation in the northeast.[38]

Countries in Western Europe:

Myanmar's relations with the West have vastly improved since the 2010 political and economic reforms. Sanctions have been lifted, and diplomatic contacts have been re-established. The US

---

[38] Prasse-Freeman, E(2017), The Rohingya Crisis, Anthropology Today, https://doi.org/10.1111/1467-8322.12389

and the European Union, in particular, have tried to put pressure on Myanmar's government to improve its treatment of Rohingya Muslims. In 2012, US President Barack Obama paid a visit to Myanmar. He spoke explicitly about the Rohingya during his visit and urged the authorities to make human rights improvements. While Myanmar's government has consented to some reforms, it has failed to carry out these pledges.[39]

5.5 MOU between the UNHCR and Myanmar on repatriation:

The Government of Myanmar communicated the names of 3,450 Rohingya refugees who have been cleared for return to Myanmar's Rakhine State to the Government of Bangladesh through their bilateral Joint Working Group on repatriation in 2019. Myanmar's participation in this process, according to the UNHCR, is a significant step toward the affirmation of Rohingya refugees' right to return.[40]

Another significant development during this time was the signing of an MOU on 5 November 1993 between Myanmar's SLORC authorities and the UNHCR to support the voluntary return and repatriation of Myanmar residents from Rakhine State who are in UNHCR-assisted camps in Bangladesh. The GOM stated that "returnees would be allowed to return to their respective places of origin" and that "after necessary verifications... will issue to all returnees the relevant identification papers with the assistance of UNHCR." "Returnees would enjoy the same freedom of movement as all other citizens in Rakhine State, in accordance with existing rules and regulations," the Myanmar authorities said. The GOM ensured UNHCR access to all returnees in Rakhine State, among other things, so that they could fulfil their responsibilities.[41]

Preparation for Mass Repatriation:

The UNHCR's signing of a Memorandum of Understanding with Myanmar completed the trio that was thought to be required to launch a substantial repatriation effort. As a result, the UNHCR presented an Operational Plan for mass repatriation on December 19, 1993. The plan's

---

[39] Amnesty international Report(2017) on Rohingya persecuted in Myanmar

[40] UNHCR(2019), *Statement of the UNHCR on Voluntary Repatriation to Myanmar,*
https://www.unhcr.org/news/press/2019/8/5d5e720a4/unhcr-statement-voluntary-repatriation-myanmar.html

[41] Crisis Group Asia Report(2017), *Myanmar's Rohingya Crisis Enters a Dangerous New Phase*, 7 December 2017

goal was to facilitate the voluntary repatriation of about 190,000 refugees at a rate of 15-18,000 refugees every month (1,500 every other day). The Operation Plan (hence referred to as the Plan) took into account UNHCR's presence in Arakan to aid with repatriation and reintegration, as well as a sufficient improvement in Myanmar's condition. It was also assumed that all refugees would choose to return, and that the GOM would welcome them all. It was agreed as part of the Operational Plan to develop trust among refugees, governments, and non-governmental organisations.[42]

Assessment of UNHCR Repatriation Procedures:

A close examination of the UNHCR's repatriation effort reveals two distinct stages. The UNHCR followed conventional repatriation procedures in the first stage, as outlined in its Guidelines on Voluntary Repatriation. During this stage, each refugee was questioned and given information about what was going on in their home country. Returning refugees must be based on an individual's freely expressed desire. This period ran from July 1994 through July 1995. Since then, UNHCR has implemented new processes in the repatriation effort, encouraging refugees to return home and replacing individual interviews with mass registration sessions. Refugees who have legitimate reasons for refusing to return will be able to express their views, and UNHCR will not register them for repatriation. At the conclusion of the procedure, their cases will be discussed. Recent operations in Sri Lanka (1987), Iraq (1991), Guatemala (1993), and Rwanda (1994) all followed same techniques (1994). [43] The new processes present a number of critical concerns that amount to a shift in repatriation policy, which the High Commissioner ultimately acknowledged in her statement to the ExCom meeting during the 46th session. "In none of these circumstances is return likely to be under optimal conditions," she said, referring to certain recent events. It will be plagued by political insecurity and economic uncertainty in many places." The High Commissioner said that returnees from exile require ongoing protection and monitoring, which adds a "new dimension to our protection responsibilities and has led us to interpret our mandate for solutions in a protection-oriented and proactive manner… we can no longer passively wait for conditions to change so that refugees can volunteer." Instead, we must actively seek to create the conditions that will allow them to return safely (emphasis added). The new method runs counter to the

---

[42] OHCHR, (6 Nov 2018) *"Myanmar: UN expert pleads for Rohingya returns to stop, fears repeat abuses may await"*, https://www.ohchr.org/en/press-releases/2018/11/myanmar-un-expert-pleads-rohingya-returns-stop-fears-repeat-abuses-may-await

[43]The Daily Star (16 March 2018), *"With Rohingya gone, Myanmar's ethnic Rakhine seek Muslim-free 'buffer zone"*, Dhaka

UNHCR's Voluntary Repatriation Guidelines and ExCom Conclusions Nos. 18 and 40. The responsibility for repatriation was shifted from individual refugees to UNHCR under the new method. In response to MSF's contribution to the ExCom meeting in 1995.[44]

As previously noted, determining the true motivation behind this abrupt shift in policy is challenging, particularly at a time when the previous system was beginning to work and provide benefits. It's possible that a number of variables came together. With a change in the Relief Commissioner in July 1994, the GOB changed its policy to allow UNHCR to do promotion sessions and interviews in all camps rather than just transit camps. The second factor could be UNHCR rethinking new ways of being proactive in repatriation preparations. This could have been motivated by the completion of repatriation preparations in Rakhine state, where UNHCR has partnered with the World Food Programme to launch an integrating aid programme. The third aspect might be seen in the draft MOU that GOB submitted to UNHCR. The Bangladesh government urged in the draft MOU that "the level of voluntariness in repatriation of Rohingya refugees be judged on the basis of the Myanmar government's current policy toward the refugees." According to the MOU, Myanmar has already recognised 135,000 of the total refugees as citizens, thus these Rohingya individuals should no longer be considered refugees and should be returned to Rakhine state as soon as feasible. According to the draught, the plan was "very compatible" with the 1951 Geneva Convention and the 1967 Protocol. (Holiday, July 29, 1994) The draft, on the other hand, was never completed. According to a high-ranking Bangladesh government source, UNHCR officials have agreed to discontinue individual interrogation of refugees and instead focus on mass registration. The fourth factor could be that the refugees decided to return because of the living conditions in the camps where they had stayed for too long, where their children were not receiving an education and where they had no economic life, and which were possibly less comfortable than in their home village.[45]

<u>5.6</u> Refugee Protection in India:

In India, the governance architecture is somewhat complicated. While the Indian Constitution makes law and order a state topic, international affairs and border control are solely the responsibility of the Union or Central Government. As a result, a number of government entities, both at the federal and state levels, have been tasked with dealing with refugee issues related to law enforcement. In addition, the Union government establishes all policies governing refugees, even if the brunt of the impact of the refugee situation must be carried to

---

[44] Myanmar: UN expert pleads for Rohingya returns to stop, fears repeat abuses may await", OHCHR, 6 November 2018

[45] Al Jazeera (Nov, 2018). *Ongoing Rohingya Repatriation efforts are doomed to failure*, Doha

a greater extent by the state administration. The contradiction between the centre and the states, as well as power-sharing relationships, have a significant impact on refugee protection inadequacies.

Despite the fact that India has hosted a huge number of refugees throughout its history, it has dealt with the challenges on a bilateral or piecemeal basis. The following are some of India's most well-known refugees: Since China's annexation in 1951, India has welcomed roughly 420,400 refugees, including 110,000 Tibetans. The ethnic civil war has displaced almost four lakh people, the majority of whom are Sri Lankan Tamils. Following the takeover of their land in 1964, about 36,000 Buddhist ethnic Chakmas and Hajongs from present-day Bangladesh fled to Arunachal Pradesh. Historically, we have hosted a large number of refugees at various times in history, including Zoroastrians and Jews during the mediaeval period, Tibetans, Sri Lankan Tamils, Burmese, East Pakistani refugees, Chittagong Hill Tracts people, Rohingyas, Somalis, Sudanese, and Nigerians.[46]

India is governed under a federal system with a Union of States. The Union legislature, i.e. the Parliament, is given exclusive authority over citizenship, naturalisation, and immigrants. India has yet to pass refugee-specific law that governs refugee entrance and status. On a political and administrative level, it has dealt with the refugees. As a result, unless a particular provision is provided, refugees are processed under Indian law that applies to aliens.

Differential treatment has been given to refugees from various nations in India. There were large refugee flows from Bangladesh, and the National Human Rights Commission provided the Chakmas with aspects of their right to life and dignity (NHRC). In comparison to other refugee groups, Tibetans received significantly better treatment. In the case of Sri Lankan Tamil refugees, an official refugee determination process was followed, and the 1951 Convention's principle of non-refoulment was followed. The 1951 Convention and the 1967 Protocol do not apply to India. Because there is no domestic legislation on the question of refugees, an individual refugee is effectively protected by the Indian Constitution. The provisions of these international treaties, on the other hand, have now been recognised as customary international law. It currently participates actively in the UNHCR-led EXCOM (Executive Committee), but has not yet ratified the 1951 Refugee Status Convention. The UNHCR frequently supports the Indian government's efforts, particularly when it comes to verifying an individual's background and the overall circumstances in their place of origin, a process known as refugee status determination (RSD). The RSD process entails the following: in order for a claimant refugee to make a valid claim for refugee status determination, the claimant must gather all the documentation he or she can in support of the grounds of persecution or fear of persecution resulting in flight from the place of origin. An identity card of employment with a governmental agency in the country of origin, or an identity card indicating membership in a particular group, are examples of acceptable documentation. The production of the same would serve as proof of a claim of involvement with specific groups as well as the claimant's identity. Any other information that the claimant can gather to prove specific persecution or fear of persecution, such as names of persecutors, leaders of groups involved in persecution, and details of areas where persecution is committed, will help

---

[46]Parivelan K. M *Reimagining refugee protection in India vis-à-vis Global Compact on Refugees* In Irudaya Rajan S in ed. The Routledge handbook of Refugees in India, Routledge, London and Newyork,2022

strengthen the claimant's case in determining the 'well founded fear' notion. Similarly, the claimant must be able to prove that all of his comments to interrogating authorities are accurate and consistent. If there are obvious inconsistencies between the claimant's statements to different people at different times, his or her claim to refugee status may be denied. The claimant's statements must also be consistent with general information about the country of origin available from media and other sources. The ability to corroborate and confirm facts about persecution is crucial in determining refugee status. The UNHCR also plays an essential role in 'durable solutions,' such as voluntary repatriation and refugee resettlement.[47]

Refugees in India are guaranteed certain Fundamental Rights under the Indian Constitution. Non-citizens, including refugees, have the same rights as citizens, including the right to equality (Article 14), the right to life and personal liberty (Article 21), the right to protection against arbitrary arrest (Article 22), the right to protection in the face of criminal convictions (Article 20), freedom of religion (Article 25), and the right to petition the Supreme Court for the enforcement of Fundamental Rights (Article 32). The refugee's human rights to live in dignity are protected by constitutional rights. Article 21 today has a liberal interpretation that encompasses the right against solitary imprisonment, the right against custodial violence, and the right to medical treatment and housing.

The United Nations General Assembly adopted the New York Declaration for Refugees and Migrants in September 2016 against the backdrop of heightened worldwide attention to refugee and migration issues. This was a watershed moment when the United Nations' 193 member states agreed on the importance of better responding to movements and enhancing the protection of all people on the move, including those fleeing armed conflict, poverty, food insecurity, persecution, terrorism, or human rights violations; those fleeing the effects of climate change and natural disasters; and those fleeing in search of new economic opportunities. From the beginning, India was actively involved in the development of the Compact. In September 2016, India spoke before the United Nations General Assembly at the passage of the New York Declaration, highlighting the problems encountered by refugees and the need for actions to address the core reasons that push them to escape. India indicated its support for the core notion of 'burden-sharing' to secure refugee protection, in addition to the non-refoulment principle, during the theme debates on the Global Compact in 2017.[48]

India is a signatory to a number of United Nations and World Conventions on Human Rights, Refugee Issues, and Related Matters, while not being a signatory to the 1951 Refugee Convention or the 1967 Protocol. As a result, its obligations to refugees are derived from the latter. India has also voted in favour of ratifying the Universal Declaration of Human Rights, which guarantees basic human rights to all people, citizens and non-citizens alike, including the right to asylum. Through the lens of the GCR, India's refugee protection can be examined or redesigned, with the potential to improve policy and practises in line with international human rights norms. Everyone wants justice, but there are a number of roadblocks in the way. The most marginalised and vulnerable groups are refugees and stateless people[49]. Aside from the 1951 Convention on the Status of Refugees and its 1967 Protocol, the 1954 Convention on

---

[47] B. S. Chimni in Field, Jessica, Burra, Srinivas (eds). *The Global Compact on Refugees: Indian Perspectives and Experiences. New Delhi: Academicians Working Group & UNHCR India*, 2020
[48] Global Compact on Refugees, United Nations, New York, 2018
[49] Global Compact on Refugee

Statelessness, and the 1961 Statelessness Reduction Convention, international laws and treaties relating to human rights and refugees include:[50]

> (a) UDHR – Articles 14 and 15: Right to seek asylum and Non-deprivation of nationality; (b) ICCPR – Articles 1 and 27: Right to self-determination and treatment of minorities; (c) ICESCR – Article 2 (3) economic rights to non-nationals; (d) SDG – Goal 16: Promoting Just, Peaceful, and Inclusive Societies In addition, the following human rights documents should be considered: (e) Four Geneva Conventions – International Humanitarian Law; (f) Convention Against Torture; (g) Child Rights Convention; (h) CEDAW.

<u>5.7</u> Mental Health of Rohingya Refugee:

As a result of prior human rights violations, including violence in Myanmar, Rohinya refugees today face harsh living conditions in Indian and Bangladeshi refugee camps. Movement limitations, a lack of livelihood options, issues meeting basic necessities, safety concerns, and limited access to services like as healthcare and education are among the challenges in the camps, as documented elsewhere. Conditions have deteriorated in recent months as a result of Covid19 and related steps to slow transmission, as well as seasonal extreme weather events creating flooding and other problems.

Mental health issues have been exacerbated by Myanmar's history of brutality and systemic human rights violations, as well as daily stressors connected with refugee living in Bangladesh. High degrees of despair, anxiety, PTSD, anger, psychosomatic symptoms, and suicide Tendency are all examples of this. Unfortunately, due to resource limits and other challenges, such as a lack of trained mental health staff who can speak the Rohingya language, there are impediments to addressing population-level mental health issues, resulting in a lack of scaled culturally relevant therapies.

As the Rohingya refugee problem has grown in size in recent years, demand has mounted to find long-term solutions. To date, the main focus has been on repatriating Rohingya refugees to Myanmar; however, as several stakeholders have pointed out, the situation is not yet favourable to a safe return. Despite this, Bangladesh and Myanmar agreed to a contentious repatriation framework, with preparations in place to repatriate the first batch of families without consulting the community or the UNHCR. These repatriation plans have been viewed as inappropriate in the present political atmosphere after the Myanmar military throw the democratic government in February 2021 making debates about the prerequisites for a safe and voluntary return all the more important.

---

[50] Parivelan K. M *Reimagining refugee protection in India vis-à-vis Global Compact on Refugees* In Irudaya Rajan S in ed. The Routledge handbook of Refugees in India, Routledge, London and Newyork,2022

BIBLIOGRAPHY AND REFERENCES:

• E. Fiddian-Qasmiyeh, G. Loescher, K. Long, and N. Sigona (2014). The Oxford Handbook of Refugee and Forced Migration Studies is a collection of essays on refugees and forced migration. Oxford University Press, London.

https://journals.sagepub.com/doi/abs/10.1177/0020702015622996

• J. Creswell (1998). Choosing Among Five Approaches to Qualitative Inquiry and Research Design Sage Publication, New Delhi.

- Parivelan K. M *Reimagining refugee protection in India vis-à-vis Global Compact onRefugees* In Irudaya Rajan S in ed. The Routledge handbook of Refugees in India, Routledge, London and Newyork,2022
- Jaha, G. (1994). *Rohingya Imbroglio: The Implication for Bangladesh,* https://jurnal.ugm.ac.id/ikat/article/view/37391
- OHCHR(2017) *Myanmar: Report of an Independent International Fact-Finding Mission,*https://www.ohchr.org/sites/default/files/Documents/HRBodies/HRCouncil/FFM-Myanmar/A_HRC_39_64.pdf
- Myanmar Politics and the Tatmadaw(2018)", Directorate of the Public Relations and Psychological Warfare, 2018, p. 116
- ICG, Myanmar: Crisis Group Asia Report N°282, 15 Dec 2016: A New Muslim Insurgency in Rakhine State
- Myanmar: IDP Sites in Rakhine State (Sep 2016), UN Office for the Coordination of Humanitarian Affairs (OCHA), 30 September 2016, available at http://www.refworld.org/docid/58343f474.html
- Amnesty international Report on Rohingya persecuted in Myanmar(2017) https://www.amnesty.org/en/latest/news/2017/10/myanmar-new-evidence-of-systematic-campaign-to-terrorize-and-drive-rohingya-out/
- Amnesty International, Myanmar(2017): *The ethnic cleansing of Rohingyas in Rakhine State is fueled by a scorched-earth operation. 2017,* https://bit.ly/2wZWZIE.
- UNHCR(2016) *Study on Community Perceptions of Citizenship, Documentation, and Rights in Rakhine State*, Myanmar
- Rakhine Commission(2017), *For The People of Rakhine, Towards a Peaceful, Fair, and Prosperous Future, Advisory Commission on Rakhine State,* https://www.rakhinecommission.org/app/uploads/2017/08/FinalReport_Eng.pdf
- ICG, Myanmar: Crisis Group Asia Report N°282, 15 Dec 2016: *A New Muslim Insurgency in Rakhine State,* https://www.crisisgroup.org/asia/south-east-asia/myanmar/283-myanmar-new-muslim-insurgency-rakhine-state
- Chaudhury Basu Ray, (2020). *The ruling of the International Court of Justice (ICJ) on the Rohingya people and its ramifications. The Observer Research Foundation provided the information for this article.*
- S. Haidar (2017, Sep 09). *The move in Bali positions India on the other side of the Rohingya issue. The following is an expert from The Hindu*
- India (2020, March 17). In the case of Indian, *Union of India vs Union Muslim League, Writ Petition (Civil) No. 1470 of 2019*
- R. Baker (2010). *Old, Challenges and New, Debates in Customary International Law in the Twenty-First Century*, (page 172-203) in The European Journal of International Law, vol. 21, no. 1.

- [1] World Food Programme (2011), *Food Security*
- *Assessment in the Northern part of Rakhine State,* Rome(Italy)
  https://documents.wfp.org/stellent/groups/public/documents/ena/wfp234781.pdf
- WHO(2009), *Child growth criteria and the detection of severe acute malnutrition in new-borns and children: a joint statement,* World Health Organization. Geneva,
  http://apps.who.int/iris/bitstream/handle/10665/44129/9789241598163_eng.pdf;jsessionid=C45DC43487FEECFB9DC7A1982F7EAE3D?sequence=1

- Nutrition Sector(2018), Emergency Nutrition Assessment: Preliminary Results (April 28 – May 28, Nutrition Sector: Cox's Bazar, Bangladesh,
  https://www.humanitarianresponse.info/sites/www.humanitarianresponse.info/files/assessments/18061 2_emergency_nutrition_assessment_round_2_ms_nyp_preliminary_results.pdf
- Charlson, F.J, *Post-traumatic stress disorder and major depression in conflict-affected populations: an epidemiological model and predictor analysis.* Global Mental Health (Camb), 2016, https://www.ncbi.nlm.nih.gov/pmc/articles/PMC5314754/
- Shanker, R., & Vijayaraghavan, H. (2020, November), *Refugee recognition challenges in India,* FMR online,https://www.fmreview.org/recognising-refugees/shanker-vijayaraghavan
- India firm on deporting Rohingya. Retrieved from The Hindu:
  https://www.thehindu.com/news/national/other-states/india-firm-on-deportingrohingya/article19625028

• L. Given (2008). The SAGE Encyclopaedia of Qualitative Research Methods is a collection of articles on qualitative research methods. Sage \sPublication. **http://sk.sagepub.com/reference/research/n398.xml**

• Bernard H. (2006). Anthropology Research Methods: Qualitative and Quantitative Approaches Altamira Press, Lamham. Retrieved \sFrom:(**http://www.dphu.org/uploads/attachements/books/books 476 0.pdf**

• B.S. Chimni (Eds). (2000). A Reader on International Refugee Laws Sage Publications, New Delhi.

• B.S. Chimni (2003). India's Refugee Status: Strategic Ambiguity R. Samaddar, R. Samaddar, R. Samaddar, R (Ed.). Refugees and the state of affairs India's Asylum and Care Practices, 1947–2000 (pp. 443–71). Sage Publications, Delhi.

• S., Guys (2007). In international law, a refugee is a person who has been forced to from their home Oxford University Press is a publishing house based in the United Kingdom.

https://books.google.co.in/books/about/The refugee in international law.html?id=A qeRAAAAMAAJ&redir esc=y&redir esc=y

• L. Drummond (1981). Culture Theory, Ethnicity, and 'Ethnicity' 693-696 in Man, 16(4), new series. **http://www.jstor.org/stable/2801497** was used to get this information.

• J. Yinger, (1985). Annual Review of Sociology, vol. 11, no. 1, pp. 151-180. **http://www.jstor.org/stable/2083290/retrieved**

• B. Anderson (1983). Communities that have been imagined. London. Verso

• T.K. Ommen(1997). From colonialism to globalisation, citizenship and national identity have been increasingly important. New Delhi is the capital of India. Publication by Sage

• K. Parivelan,(2013). Protection requirements, existing legal avenues, and new legal and strategic options: A South Asian viewpoint. Anxious States, Unstable Population: In South Asia, there are both mixed and massive population migrations. Paula Banerjee is the editor. Samya is a publishing house based in India.

73 Journal Articles, Reports, and Documents:

-

• Refugee Facts from the UNHCR, **https://www.unrefugees.org/refugee-facts/what-is-a-refugee/**

• Internal Displacement, IDMC, http://www.internal-displacement.org/internaldisplacement/internaldisplacement/internaldisplacement/internaldisplacement/internaldisplacement/internaldisplacement/

• What is Statelessness?, a UNHCR report, https://www.unhcr.org/ibelong/wpcontent/uploads/UNHCR-Statelessness-2pager-ENG.pdf

• The United Nations High Commissioners for Refugees' guidebook, Representing Stateless Persons Before US Immigration Authorities: A Legal Practice Resource, **https://www.unhcr.org/statelessness.html**

• The BBC (April, 2018). What you need to know about the Rohingya situation in Myanmar. BBC. **https://www.bbc.com/news/world-asia-41566561**

• S. Vishwanathan (2017). Every one of us contains a Rohingya. The Hindu is a Hindu religion. **http://www.thehindu.com/opinion/lead/there-is-a-rohingya-in-every-one-of-us/article19626127.ece**

• Human Rights Watch is an organisation that monitors human rights violations (2017). By the River, there was a massacre. **http://www.hrw.org/report/2017/12/19/massacre-river/burmese-army-crimes-against-humanity-tula-toli/**

• Albert, E. (Dec, 2018). The Rohingya Refugee Crisis The Council on Foreign Relations is a non-profit organisation that promotes international cooperation Backgrounder on the Rohingya situation can be found at **https://www.cfr.org/backgrounder/rohingya-crisis.**

• S.M. Khasaru(2017). Next door's disaster. The Hindu is a Hindu religion. **www.thehindu.com/todays-paper/tp-opinion/the-disaster-next-door/article19657443.ece**

• U. Singh (2018). The National Human Rights Commission of India is a 'inside-outside' body. The Economic and Political Weekly is a weekly publication that focuses on economic and political issues.

• Staff of the Wire (April, 2018). In Delhi, a Rohingya camp has been reduced to ashes. The Wire is a drama series set in the United States. Retrieved from https://thewire.in/government/delhi-rohingya-camp-burned-to-ashes

• J. William (2008). Observation by a non-participant. Nonparticipant observation was retrieved from **https://www.researchgate.net/publication/265280500 Nonparticipant observation.**

L. Drummond, L. Drummond, L. Drummond, L. Drummond (1981). Culture Theory, Ethnicity, and 'Ethnicity' 693-696 in Man, 16(4), new series. 74 http://www.jstor.org/stable/2801497

• Human Rights Watch is an organisation that monitors human rights violations (2017). Report on the World. https://www.hrw.org/world-report-2018/country-chapters/burma#73fccc

• A. Phillips (2013). Shedding Light on the Persecuted, the World's Blind Spot

31-33 in Harvard International Review, vol. 35, no. 2. http://www.jstor.org/stable/42763572 retrieved

• J. Ferguson (2015). Who's keeping track? Ethnicity, Belonging, and Burma/National Myanmar's Census 171(1), 1-28 in Bijdragen Tot De Taal-, Land-, en Volkenkunde.

http://www.jstor.org/stable/43819166 retrieved

H. Habib, (2017). It is Bangladesh's responsibility to bear this load. The Hindu is a Hindu religion. http://www.thehindu.com/opinion/op-ed/rohingya-bangladesh-burden-to-bear/article19694058.ece

• H. Pant (2017). In Myanmar, India's balancing act. The Diplomat is a fictional character. https://thediplomat.com/2017/09/india-s-balancing-act-in-Myanmar/ .

• K. Das (Jan, 2019). After being deported, hundreds of Rohingya families have fled India.

Hundreds of Rohingya families escape India after deportations, according to https://in.reuters.com/article/myanmar-rohingya-india/hundreds-offrohingya-families-flee-india-after-deportations-idINKCN1PB1G7

Staff who scrolls. (January 2019) Five Rohingyas were deported to Myanmar from an Assam prison. http://scroll.in/latest/908187/five-rohingyas-lodged-in-assam-prison-deported-to-myanmar

• According to Reuters (Jan, 2019).

Today, India will deport a second group of Rohingya Muslims to Myanmar.

http://www.businesstoday.in/current/economy-politics/india-to-deport-second-rohingya-group-to-myanmar-today/story/306424.html

• Go to the Knowledge Platform for the United Nations Sustainable Development Goals. https://sustainabledevelopment.un.org/topics/sustainabledevelopmentgoals.html

P. Gottschlich, Gottschlich, Gottschlich, Gottschlich, Gottschlich (2017). After a change of government, will the India-Myanmar relationship take new directions? http://asianstudies.arnoldbergstraesser.de/sites/default/files/field/afdownload/iqas india myanmar gottschlich.pdf

• The Reuters news agency (2018). China claims that the Rohingya refugee crisis should not be 'internationalised.'

http://www.reuters.com/article/us-myanmar-rohingya-china/chinasays-rohingya-issue-shouldnt-be-internationalized-idUSKCN1M8062

• The United States Intellectual Property Office (USIP) (Sep, 2018). The Role of China in Myanmar's Internal Conflicts https://**www.usip.org/publications/2018/09/chinas-role-in-internal-conflicts-in-Myanmar**

75

• Md. Noor (Jan, 2018). The Rohingya Crisis and Bangladesh's Concerns Retrieved \sFrom: \shttps://www.researchgate.net/publication/322222196 Rohingya Crisis and The Con \scerns for Bangladesh

Documents Legal:

• 1951 Convention on the Status of Refugees

 • Myanmar Citizenship Law of 1984

ANNEXURE

SEMI-STRUCTURED INTERVIEW SCHEDULE (For Rohingya Refugees)

Name:_______________/Informant No.____(If Confidential)

Venue: _______________

Date: _______________

Time: _______________

Demography Details

1. Agency Associated with (if any):_______________________________

2. Date of Birth/Age: _______________

3. Sex: Male______/ Female_________

4. Place of Birth: _______________

5. Country of Origin/Nationality_________________

6. Ethnicity: _______________

7. Religion: ___________________________

8. Language Spoken: _________________

9. Education: _______________________

10. No of Siblings: _________________

11. Marital status: _________________

12. Do you have children, and if so, how many?

13. Are You feeling safe here?

14. How much money did you make in Myanmar?

15. Do you have a job in India right now?

16. What are your responsibilities here?

17. What is your monthly income?

18. What is your daily working hour?

19. Do you get good treatment at work?

20. Are you free to go around the city?

Reason For Migration:

1. What country were you born in?

2. Why and when did you decide to move? What led to your decision to move? Have there been any other people in your neighbourhood who have left?

3. Do you have access to basic necessities in Myanmar, such as education, housing, health, and other social services?

4. How frequently did the tense situation erupt? What was your reaction?

5. Do you have any touch with someone in Myanmar? If no, please explain why.

6. What exactly do you mean when you say "citizenship"?

7. What differences did you notice before and after the Myanmar Citizenship Act was enacted?

Migration:

1. With whom did you travel? What mode(s) of transport did you employ? Is it true that individuals in your neighbourhood have left? Who went and who stayed?

2. Who did you go with? What items did you bring with you?

3. What happened on the way there? What did you come up with in the end?

4. What made you believe that visiting India was a viable option?

5. What is the difference between the scenario when you migrated and the current situation? Do you believe India's position has improved?

6. Who or what is the primary source of forced migration?

India's Current Situation and Future Securities:

1. What obstacles did you face in establishing a new way of life in India?
What steps did you take to overcome them?

2. Have you received any official documentation from the Indian government, the UNHCR?

3. How safe do you feel in India? Please tell us about your experience.

4. What do you hope to achieve from India's government?

5. How do you see the Rohingya's future in India?

6. Do you intend to return to Myanmar?
If not, why not?

7. What level of assistance do you anticipate from Myanmar's government?

8. What role should India play in ensuring the safe return of refugees?

9. Do you have any photos or mementos of violence or transit? Could you please share these with me?

10. Do you have anything else you'd want to say?